PEDALS *and* PETTICOATS

On the road in post-war Europe

Mary Elsy

summersdale

PEDALS AND PETTICOATS

Summersdale Publishers Ltd
46 West Street
Chichester
West Sussex
PO19 1RP
UK

www.summersdale.com

Printed and bound in Great Britain

ISBN 1 84024 439 9

Mary Elsy is a travel writer and journalist, and the author of six books. She lives in London.

CONTENTS

PART ONE

1

PREPARATIONS AND STARTING OFF

We were four – Agnes, Barbara, Esme and myself. Our immediate destination was Belgium, then most of Western Europe: Luxembourg, Germany, Austria, Italy, Spain and France, all to be visited with bikes and a tent.

Our journey had been Barbara's idea and had seemed to come to her out of the blue. My sister had always been a romancer. She was rather a beauty, plumpish but with a Spanish look about her. I, her younger by a few years, was thin, almost skinny. We got on fairly well with just the occasional spat that sisters sometimes have. Barbara had suddenly come out with, 'Let's do a tour of Europe,' adding, as if it were the most natural way to travel, 'We'll cycle camp.'

We were in the sitting room of our rather shabby flat in Finchley Road, Hampstead, that we shared with our brother Gordon. Ceilings had come down and windows blown in during the buzz bombs raids, and though they had been rapidly repaired at the time, they had been makeshift jobs. No decorating had been done for years. People didn't bother so much about such things. It might all be messed up again after a raid. They could count themselves lucky to have a home that was still habitable.

Our father was a well-known and successful photographer between the wars. He owned a large business elsewhere on Finchley Road, which sometimes employed as many as thirty people. Our mother managed the business thus leaving him free to concentrate on the artistic side. It was quite an exciting place to grow up in. There was a lift, indoor telephones, a large studio full of props, and even a small cinema where my father showed 'Felix the Cat' films to children who had just been photographed. Our home was above the business. As we had no garden we played on the roof, which was quite safe as it was surrounded by railings. It was decorated with boxes of flowers, and there were benches and a table where we sometimes ate our evening meal. A corrugated iron hut on one side, once used for drying prints, was taken over by Barbara and me as a summer bedroom. On very hot nights, we would drag our mattresses outside and sleep under the stars.

Our father later became ill and died not long before the Second World War. It was fortunate for him in a way as the building was blasted during the blitz, destroying part of the library opposite, so he did not see the destruction of his life's work. Thankfully, we were staying with some friends that night. Unable to live there any longer, my mother (rescuing what furniture she could and storing it with friends), Barbara and I evacuated ourselves to Taunton, Somerset to stay with an uncle and aunt. My brother Gordon was then in the army.

However, like many Londoners, my mother disliked provincial life and, using an old business contact, rented a somewhat dilapidated flat above two shops in Finchley Road. It was not very far from our old business, now boarded up and uninhabitable. There had been a lull in the bombing of London and the city now seemed relatively safe.

Our mother, although spirited (she had been a suffragette) was not very strong. The loss of our father, our business and livelihood, and the bombing had worn her out. Buzz bombs (buzzing pilotless planes) would drop suddenly and silent rockets gave no warning but did enormous damage. She died after the war in early 1950.

The idea of the trip had come to Barbara not long after Christmas 1950, when she'd been leafing her way through an old school atlas. Most of the colourful brochures advertising holidays abroad had yet to come. Much of Europe, still very damaged by the war, was a place to speak of rather than visit. England, also, was fairly grim. Churchill, our great war leader, had been toppled and the Labour party, under Atlee, was in power. Food provisions were low and many things such as paper were in short supply. Few books were being published and magazines and newspapers were thin. Clothes, like food, had been rationed. Now we had the 'New Look', a utility style, but more feminine with long skirts and jackets. I suppose this was a reaction to the uniforms worn by girls in the forces. Hair styles were getting longer, too. Girls working in the factories or the forces were not supposed to let their hair fall below their collar.

Barbara had a small administrative job with a local authority. As well as being keen on art and something of a painter, she was interested in social work; maybe a sort of amateur study of living conditions abroad at this time was another reason for her wanting to do the trip. She had taken a social science diploma after studying in the evenings and was planning to go on a year's course to train as a youth employment officer in September.

I had taken a teaching diploma after the war and done a few years' teaching, but had hankerings of becoming a journalist. I had planned to take some exercise books along with me so I could write up a diary as we went along.

Agnes, who'd come for the evening, was sitting on the edge of a stool. She always sat on the edge of things as if she were afraid of being too comfortable. She was a very tall blonde and, like us, in her twenties. She was idealistic, loved causes, and a great enthusiast once she got going, which was lucky for us. She worked for Federal Union, an organisation which wanted Britain to become part of a united Europe, something the then Labour government was loath to do. It was usually short of money so probably wouldn't mind allowing a member of the staff some unpaid leave.

Barbara and I had met Agnes through the Garret Club, a small club for people interested in the arts, which Barbara and I had joined. Oonah, its enthusiastic founder, was anxious to expand it, and decided to hold a dance (charging an entrance fee) in conjunction with Federal Union, whose staff was always trying to raise money. Thus we met Agnes, its secretary, who became an eager member of the Garret Club. We would meet in each others' homes, holding discussions and readings of our story-writing efforts, and also go on excursions to interesting places. Agnes soon became a firm friend of ours.

Barbara's idea met with a cool reception at first from Agnes and me. Agnes, an experienced cyclist, foresaw innumerable difficulties. However, we three discussed the project, saying first that it was really impossible – or nearly – but a nice idea, even so. We hadn't enough money, although maybe we would be able to collect enough by early summer. Agnes's family had a tent we might use. A scheme evolved very gradually. It expanded into a proper plan. Our imaginations were gripped. It would be a terrific adventure – a test of what girls could achieve and of their ingenuity and endurance.

We had met Esme through our mothers who were both women Rotarians (the Inner Wheel, it was called) and who became friends as they lived near each other. That Esme came with us was more or less chance. Barbara met her not long after suggesting the tour and mentioned the idea to her. She was just coming out of our local grocer, Sprotts, in Finchley Road, having just given our weekly order, and Esme was passing by. Sprotts was old-fashioned and dark but sold most of what you wanted. It gave a personal service, delivering one's order without charge.

Esme was a few years younger than us and in her first job, which was secretarial, dull and juniorish. There weren't many interesting jobs for girls at that time, even if they had a degree. The choices seemed to be limited to nursing, teaching, secretarial or maybe the civil service. The economy was still in the doldrums, had not yet expanded, and we were still paying for the war. Girls were expected to marry and have children. Not so easy to do then as so many potential husbands had been killed in the war.

Esme, an only child, perhaps over-protected, was certainly not used to roughing it. I think she thought it would be an exciting escape from a dull English existence. We others thought it would be nice to have her company. Also, her cycle would be an extra one on which to carry our equipment.

Although the idea had been Barbara's, it seemed that the having of it was of itself sufficient. It was Agnes, so scornful at first, who took upon herself most of the planning and preparations. She came from an enterprising but not very well-off family. 'Make do and mend' had always been very much part of their lives, as it had been for most people during and to some extent after the war. Her father was a keen camper and also an amateur naturalist, so the family had been brought up to love camping and exploring the countryside. Rumour had it that Agnes had just missed being born in a tent. So she had the know-how and also, most usefully, was able to provide most of the equipment.

The tent, old-fashioned even in the 1950s, was made of a very thin Egyptian cotton and had light bamboo poles to support it. These could be taken apart and strapped in bags to the sides of the two machines. Our tent pegs were old meat skewers. Our towels, for lightness, were made out of butter muslin. Agnes lent us each a sleeping bag, which could be rolled up and carried in our panniers. Our sheets had a real World War Two flavour. They were made out of a large orange parachute I bought from a shop in the Strand selling disused war materials. Barbara and I took a junior-sized Lilo each. Agnes, because she was tough, and Esme, possibly because she wanted to appear so, stoutly asserted that they would sleep on the ground. We took few clothes, but

13

strong walking shoes were a must. We knew there would be plenty of times when we'd have to push our bikes.

As we knew we'd have to store our food as we went along, Barbara said she would put our day-to-day purchases in her front basket. We bought a few things, such as a packet of tea, sugar, salt and a tin of sardines for emergencies, which could be kept in a long black basket strapped on one carrier. This would also contain four plastic mugs, a folding saucepan, a collapsible Primus stove, a tea-infuser, water bags, knives, forks, spoons, tin plates and a receptacle for carrying our milk in. We all joined the Youth Hostel Association, which meant we'd have somewhere to stay cheaply if we couldn't use the tent.

We were each allocated a particular job. Barbara, who was in charge of catering in our flat, was made cook. Agnes and Esme agreed to be responsible for putting up and taking down the tent. Agnes was also to be puncture-mender. I, who tended to be argumentative and could look quite fierce when annoyed, was appointed treasurer. 'People would be less likely to cheat her,' Agnes said. We were to take £65 each, which we hoped would last us the tour.

Barbara and I had some difficulty in persuading our brother that he would be all right if left on his own. Apart from the fact that he would have to do his own cooking and washing, he was also planning to marry at the end of August.

'Mind you're back in time,' Gordon warned Barbara and me, as we'd both been earmarked to be bridesmaids. We reassured him that there was little need to worry. It was unlikely that our money would last much longer then eight or nine weeks.

We had already let out our mother's room after she'd died to two Canadian girls, Joan and Irene. Joan worked in the personnel department of a large London store. In fact, it was the same firm at which Gordon's fiancée worked, and it was Joan who had introduced them. Irene worked in accountancy. Joan came with us on a trial run to Oxford before the tour, but gave up halfway and returned home by train. 'No wonder you Brits win all your wars,' she told us wearily. 'Your women are so tough.'

June 11 was D-Day. The day on which our mini invasion of Europe began.

As Esme lived close to Barbara and me, the three of us began the tour rather grandly in Esme's parents' car. We had ridden our bikes to Victoria station the previous evening and left them there, and so only had our equipment to worry about. Esme's mother, who was half-Italian, was still fretting about her daughter going on such a nebulous expedition, so the atmosphere in the car was rather strained. However, her father, who had once lived in Canada and had been a rolling stone himself before going into business, treated the tour as if it were a great joke. I think he was also rather proud of her. He was chiefly concerned that she should have enough money and about what she should do if she ran out. Esme had left her job, which she'd been planning to do anyway.

We found Agnes and her father waiting at the station. They'd come up from the suburbs where they lived by train. He had great confidence in Agnes's capabilities.

The three parents waved us off. My last sight was of Esme's and Agnes's fathers laughing together and Esme's mother looking fearful. Her final words to Esme had been, 'Come home if you get tired – and write, write, write...'

Lines flashed by as we waved goodbye. We passed a signal box, rows of sooty houses, railway sheds, yards filled with scrap, workmen drinking mugs of tea. We were off at last. The great adventure had started. Our gypsy life had begun.

We all felt nervous although we didn't admit it to each other. What would happen to us in the coming months? What sort of a reception would we receive from our old enemies, Germany and Italy? We'd none of us been abroad much before. Travel during the war had mostly been restricted to the forces. Barbara and I had made a short trip to Switzerland in 1949, and Agnes had gone camping in Germany just before the war.

At Dover, our bikes had to be stripped of our possessions before being put in the hold below. We had to struggle up on deck with our equipment and then deposit it all in an untidy pile.

It did not seem long before we were at sea, with the wind blowing in our faces. The crossing to Ostend was easy in spite of the wind. There was a warm sun overhead: the sea around us was dotted with crafts, mostly fishing boats, and numerous squalling seagulls. I, the treasurer, kept our money in a secret purse attached to a belt, which I wore beneath my windjammer. I stood on deck watching the horizon, while Agnes, ever friendly and unable to be silent for long, had got into conversation with Harry, a lone bespectacled cyclist from Manchester.

'He says he can help us work out Belgian currency,' she called to me cheerfully as the two of them went down to the cabin below. I followed them, greatly relieved, as I was no mathematician and was beginning to feel very apprehensive as to how I was going to work out all the different currencies we were likely to encounter. Harry, a keen cyclist, was well-travelled, and an expert on currencies. Not only was he able to give me a breakdown on Belgian money, but also on German marks.

Up on deck again, we all felt thrilled when Ostend, with its church spires, rows of tall houses and wide beach, came into view. However, our excitement soon gave way to weariness as we pushed down the gangway, again overburdened by panniers and baskets. We clung tightly to them as if they contained gold and silver and tried to ignore the blue-overalled porters who seemed so anxious to snatch them away. Harry was still with us, glad of our company, I guess.

Once on shore we watched our bikes being unloaded out of the hold. First came Agnes's, probably a hand-me-down and seemingly just holding together. Then came Barbara's and mine, sturdily built. Esme's came last. It was a brand new one – probably the latest model – which her father had recently bought her. Whatever Esme did or did not do, he was determined she would have a good machine beneath her. However, all that glitters is not gold, as we were to find out.

Harry's was a bright red, many-gadgeted racer. He finally left us after he'd retrieved it. He intended, probably wisely, to cycle across flat Holland.

After we'd been through customs – which itself was quite an experience, as we were not yet used to managing our bikes and baggage and showing passports at the same time – we clambered aboard the train to Brussels. Neither were we used to organising bikes and equipment for train journeys. In fact, we had only just managed to do everything that was necessary and find ourselves four window seats when the train started to move out of the station. We were exhausted and exhilarated. We had got ourselves this far and were now truly launched on the first stage of what was to be a stupendous 3,000-mile journey across western Europe.

2

BRUSSELS

Agnes, who seemed to have an inexhaustible supply of energy, was the first to recover from our exertions of catching the train. Fortunately for her, in spite of her large conscience, she was a happy-go-lucky sort of girl: leadership didn't sit too heavily upon her. A foreign member of Federal Union, visiting the organisation's London offices, had once described her as a 'tall girl, light-headed'. Although he hadn't quite meant what he said, we other three thought that this description fitted her rather well when she told us.

'I hope Georges will be at Brussels to meet us,' she said. Her tone was optimistic although she looked slightly worried.

Georges was the cousin of a friend of hers. His mother was a Yorkshire woman, who had married a Belgian and now lived in a village not far from the French frontier. Georges was in his early twenties and worked for a firm in Brussels which exported rubber. Agnes had written to him telling him what time we'd arrive.

To our great relief, Georges was waiting on the station platform when the train drew in. He had been brought up in Belgium but had often stayed with relatives in England, so he was bilingual and spoke English with a strong but warmly comforting north country accent. In fact, to us he seemed to be more English than continental. Not, of course, that we really knew much about continentals. His manner was rather shy and diffident. I expect he felt embarrassed at having to deal with four girls at once.

A smiling, rather gushing Agnes introduced us three to him quickly.

'The three adventurers,' he said politely, shaking hands, then adding quickly, 'I've booked you all in at the YWCA.'

This was some comfort to us. In spite of our careful preparations, we didn't feel like camping just yet. It would have been too much all at once even if we had managed to find a campsite near the city. However, we still had the task of transporting ourselves plus bikes and equipment to the YWCA. Loading our machines with gear was still quite a difficulty for us.

Georges proved very useful here. We didn't yet dare to ride our heavily-laden contraptions through the traffic. Even so, we soon discovered that wheeling them was almost as dangerous with all the cars, lorries, motorbikes and long cream-coloured trams clattering past. Georges led the way with Agnes, talking away, just behind.

Georges turned to Barbara, Esme and myself occasionally, first telling us to remember that traffic here drove down a different side of the road to traffic in England; then to warn me to take more care when my black basket, not strapped on properly, slid off my bike and nearly under the wheels of a passing lorry.

He also took time to point out a few places of interest, such as the Palais de Justice, whose classic dome rode high above the city's rooftops. But the four of us were too busy looking after ourselves and our precarious vehicles to pay much attention to the city's sights.

'Here we are,' he said at last. The YWCA was a tall, grey-shuttered, balconied building in the rue Jourdain. 'I won't come in.' Then, turning to leave, visibly relieved that he'd done his duty, he added: 'I'll see you outside in two hours.'

When we met him again two hours later, he seemed to have lost his shy brusqueness. Perhaps it was because it was now evening and Brussels was ablaze with bright lights. The cafés and restaurants were filling up with people. Perhaps, too, it was because we had now changed into feminine dresses – the only ones we'd allowed ourselves to bring – and were washed and tidied. He no longer had the embarrassment of accompanying four rather dirty and windswept cycle-campers.

At any rate he now behaved as we expected worldly, sophisticated continentals to behave. He was the Belgian gallant: he insisted on shaking each one of us by the hand. 'I'm proud to be the escort of four such daring young women,' he declared.

We all boarded one of the long, rattly trams. Georges took us first to see the floodlit market-place, the Grand'Place, one of Europe's most important town squares, so he told us. By day, its centre was filled with bright-hued flower stalls. Now that it was evening the large cobblestoned area acted as a car park.

Georges seemed very knowledgeable about his city, although I, somewhat sceptical, suspected that he'd probably just looked up his information in a guidebook. When I noticed that the door and the tower of the Town Hall were not in the centre as one would expect, he had the answer off pat. 'This was deliberate because the building was constructed at different times. A later architect wanted to preserve the entrance gate to the old belfry, so he was unable to make the perspective of the building uniform.'

This led him to give a little lecture about the town square, where, it appeared, much of the history of Brussels and the Low Countries had taken place. 'It was here that princes read out edicts; that the oaths of allegiance to rulers were taken; and that public executions were held.'

Unfortunately, our interest was flagging. I was staring at a fireman adjusting a flagpole atop another building, the Maison du Roi. Agnes disliked towns and wasn't much interested in history. Esme was adjusting her new sandals, which were beginning to pinch her feet. Only Barbara seemed to be listening, but as so often happened, she had disappeared behind her eyes, her thoughts wandering off, probably romancing.

'Tch!' Georges clicked his tongue, exasperated, then told us to follow him out of the square, down side-turnings and streets, until we emerged breathlessly into the rue de l'Etuve to see Mannekin Pis – a fountain, but shaped like a small boy relieving himself.

We tried to make the appropriate noises of amusement and surprise for Georges's benefit, then listened as he launched into another lecture.

'This is Brussels' oldest inhabitant. He was erected by a rich merchant as a thanksgiving. His young son, lost for four days, was found here performing.'

We nodded in encouragement.

'There is another legend that a boy put out a fire in this way,' he added. 'He is also the city's mascot and reflects its changing fortunes. Although occupying armies sometimes kidnapped him, he was always returned. On one occasion, when the populace had rioted, the French king offered him back complete with a brocade coat and the cross of St Louis, an important decoration to wear. Since then, he has worn the uniform of every occupying force, even the RAF at the end of the last war. Mannekin has hundreds of suits, all kept in the Maison du Roi.'

By the time Georges had finished recounting this last piece of information, his throat was quite dry. He led the four of us to a café in the broad Boulevard Anspach.

'I shan't be able to see you again in Brussels,' he told us. He suggested we cycle to his parents' home, which lay not far off our route, towards Luxembourg. 'I go home there every weekend by train.'

He drew a map out of his pocket, then sketched out a route for us on a page from his notebook while we drank our coffee.

'Namur, Dinant, Baronville, Bouillon, Florenville, then on towards Virton. It's about a hundred and ninety kilometres.

You should be able to get there by Friday evening.'

'It will be our first goal.' Agnes was optimistic.

Although we were still untried cycle-campers, it did not seem a very difficult feat – on paper at any rate.

'Today's Tuesday, so it will be three days' ride,' I put in. We decided that we should be able to make it.

Georges returned us to the YWCA only just in time. The tall brown doors were about to be locked for the night.

'*Bon voyage,*' he called to us from the roadway as we hastily ran inside. 'We'll meet again – perhaps,' we heard him shout.

3

FIRST NIGHT UNDER CANVAS

Agnes and I went shopping together for provisions the following morning. We planned to start on our journey in the early afternoon.

We all felt it rather a wrench that we had to leave Brussels so soon. We were beginning to get used to it, beginning to feel established and at home. And those cake shops! We pushed our faces up against their glass windows. How our stomachs ached as we smelled the seductive aroma of fresh baking. Belgium, which had adopted a free economic policy after the war, had recovered more swiftly from the war's devastation than other European nations. Unlike in Britain, there was no rationing. Brussels, an important HQ for the allied forces at the end of the war, had been a popular leave centre. Luckily for the fate of our tour and our financial situation, Agnes's austere upbringing had made her strong-minded about making sacrifices. If it had been left to us other three, we would probably have got no further than Brussels. We would each have got through our £65 allowance in an orgy of eating. Even I who, as treasurer, should have known better.

The shop Agnes chose when she and I were to buy our first day's rations must have been one of the shabbiest, dingiest little shops in the whole of Brussels.

She consulted the list that she and Barbara – our cook – had made earlier.

'We want biscuits and bread,' she began.

'And butter and chocolates and cheese and oranges... and

sausages,' I put in as she walked round the shop peering critically into the smeared glass cases below the counter. The woman behind it stared at us bewildered.

'No, only cheese. And perhaps oranges in case we get thirsty.' She was determined that we be economical.

'*Fromage, s'il vous plaît – à bon marché.*' Agnes was quite good at reading and understanding French but less good at pronunciation. However, her friendly smile and apparent poverty so disarmed the woman that she removed a piece of cheese from behind one glass case and held it up for us both to examine closely.

'*C'est le meilleur marché – ça vous plaît? Je vous ajoute quelques morceaux de biscuits, vous êtes une brave fille.*'

'*Oui, oui. Vous êtes très gentille.*'

'She's going to throw in some broken biscuits with the cheese,' she told me enthusiastically, as if she'd won a prize.

The ensuing conversation between her and the shopkeeper was animated and accompanied by many gestures. Their transaction was finally sealed by the three of us feeding a mangy, sniffling dog, which suddenly appeared from behind the counter, with some of the broken biscuits.

Our departure from the YWCA took place in the early afternoon. After we'd set our bikes in the gutter alongside the narrow, dusty pavement, Agnes walked up and down beside us, giving us last minute instructions, and tightening the strings and straps that held the panniers and baskets in place.

We were all keyed up with excitement, also a little scared. Each of us had been nearly killed at least once while trying to cross streets in Brussels, so we could not help wondering what would happen when we actually joined ourselves on to the stream of high-speed cars, lorries, trams, motorcycles and bicycles that made up the traffic on the Belgian roads.

'*Bon voyage!*' A white-haired woman, wearing the inevitable black dress that all older women in Belgium seemed to wear, leaned out of an upstairs window. She gave us a friendly wave as we wobbled precariously down the street.

It was the first time we had cycled carrying all our kit. Our machines felt unusually heavy and unwieldy as we carefully negotiated our way into the Boulevard de Waterloo.

We had to find our way out of Brussels, not so easy when we had to ask the directions in a foreign tongue. Agnes, naturally leading, managed to make a bearded Belgian cyclist understand what she needed to know, then shouted to us to follow her.

So we did, or tried to. Esme raced after her, and Barbara and I made to do the same. Unfortunately, the string bag containing the oranges chose that moment to break loose from Barbara's handlebars. A shower of golden fruit bounced over the road. By the time she and I had managed to rescue them from underneath cars and around people's feet, Esme, Agnes and the bearded Belgian were tiny dots in the distance.

Fortunately, the Belgian authorities had provided a cycle path in the centre of the road beneath cool and shady chestnut trees. Barbara and I were able to strain after them without too much danger. Eventually, panting and breathless, we caught up with Agnes and Esme at the end of the cycle-track, where the Belgian had left them.

And here, we decided, was the actual spot where our tour of Europe really started. Here, on this particular stretch of road, now occupied by screeching, rushing, terrifying traffic.

'Come on!' Agnes bravely led the way again. We other three plunged on after her, rather as if we were diving into the sea. We even wanted to close our eyes. How well I now understood why street horses wore blinkers.

We weren't able to take in much of the scenery on that first day's ride. We did not dare take our eyes off the road for long. A perspiring Esme, struggling to guide her heavily-loaded vehicle, was so intent on keeping in close to the roadside that she didn't notice a black-uniformed policeman on a motorbike swerving beside her, until he barked, '*Où allez-vous, Mademoiselle?*'

She turned a fraction to smile nervously, but was too intent on balancing the load behind her, while keeping her eyes on the road, to take in what he was saying. '*Non compris, Monsieur.*' She gave an expressive shrug of despair that nearly unbalanced her, and waved him on to Agnes.

'He was quite friendly, really,' Agnes told her when we others caught up with her and he had ridden off. 'He only wanted to know where we were going. And – what is wrong with your bike? Your legs are hardly moving at all.'

'I'm moving them as fast as I can,' a struggling Esme angrily informed her.

However, Agnes was right about the bike. Also the policeman, who turned out to be very friendly indeed. About half an hour later, when Esme's bike had almost seized up, he swerved back, this time with a chum, as if he'd been expecting this to happen. To our surprise – and immense gratitude – the two of them mended her machine at the side of the road.

This hold-up caused us to lose a lot of time. We tried to make up for it by cycling as far and as fast as we could before it became too dark to see.

Alas, we had left things too late. When at last we decided we should start to look for a suitable campsite, we discovered that much of the surrounding countryside was either too cultivated or too built-up to camp on. Also, although Brussels had appeared so affluent and prosperous, much of the outlying area was still dilapidated and shabby from the effects of the war.

We finally drew up near a dingy, pink-washed farmhouse standing some distance back from the road. Its surroundings looked neglected and overgrown. A few thin chickens fluttered around a smelly midden heap in a muddy yard, not far from the front door.

Agnes knocked on it bravely, leaving Barbara, Esme and me behind in the roadway, holding the bikes. The door was opened fairly quickly by a little old lady, rather witch-like in appearance. She wore a tattered red shawl across her shoulders. She smiled at Agnes and us three behind, revealing blackened stumpy teeth.

'*Nous avons une tente. Est-ce que c'est possible nous installer dans votre champ, s'il vous plaît?*' we heard Agnes ask in her best French.

'*Oui, oui.*' The old lady nodded. Our relief was great. We were so tired. Barbara, Esme and myself began to wheel our machines through a gate into a field beyond. At once, the old lady's friendly '*oui*'s turned into agitated '*non*'s.

'She says we must camp by the roadside.' Agnes translated her excited stream of words. 'She says there are beasts in the prairie,' she called after us.

'Prairie – I hope we're on the right continent,' I muttered as we returned to where we'd been before. The old lady, now much calmer, called upstairs to her two daughters. They joined her; as did a small girl, wearing a torn jersey and a ragged skirt, a grandchild perhaps; and a very thin dog.

But why, the old lady asked, puzzled, why did we want to sleep in a tent when there were so many good beds about?

'Because... *nous campeurs*, er, *nous aimons liberté*... er... *plein air*,' Agnes struggled to explain while Barbara, Esme and myself endeavoured to straighten the tent and knock in the tent pegs.

'*Oui, oui.*' The old lady remained doubtful, like her family, and unconvinced.

Then she came over to us and felt the tent. '*La tente a l'air bien*,' she said encouragingly, but she thought we would all be cold by morning.

4

TOWARDS PROFONDVILLE

Our first night under canvas was not very comfortable. We had yet to master the technique of sleeping four in a row, wedged tight together. There was only just room for the four of us inside when we were all lying down. This meant that as soon as the first one had made her bed, she had to climb into it, while the second one made hers, and so on.

I, the last, found that I had barely room to lie on my side even.

'It's a good thing I'm thin,' I muttered as I struggled to push myself down.

The other three shuffled closer to give me more room, difficult to do once inside their bags, and disturbing their own arrangements. Barbara and I had blown up our Lilos too full, so we felt as if we were lying on balloons, which might suddenly pop. But our bodies were too close to pull out the stoppers and deflate them. Agnes and Esme, sleeping on the ground, managed better. Agnes had collected a pile of straw from the orchard behind the farmhouse, which she placed under their side of the ground sheet.

However, we were all too tired not to fall asleep quickly and felt little inclination to rise early the next morning. It took Barbara quite a while to cook our breakfast of fried eggs, which I'd bought at the farm, and for all of us to eat them, take down the tent and load all our baggage once more on the four bikes. By the time we'd shaken hands with the old lady, who had come out to see us off, and thanked her for letting us use her land, it was past eleven.

By now, we'd worked out the best way to pack our equipment. As Agnes had the largest panniers on her bike, she kept the tent, fly-sheet, pegs and groundsheet in it. Perched above the panniers was the cooking utensil box, and balanced above that was a small canvas bag, containing her personal belongings. Esme, Barbara and I carried the bedding, the Primus stove, all our clothes and some of Agnes's in our panniers and in the basket boxes which we balanced above these. Barbara and Esme shared the tent poles – they each had one long bag strapped to one side of their machines. Barbara's front basket, intended originally to carry day-to-day food purchases, was also used for a variety of overflow articles, such as cameras.

We were slowly getting used to the traffic, which continued to whizz by, noisy, bad-tempered, aggressive. In fact, we were just beginning to enjoy the freedom of our life on the road when Esme's bike started to give her trouble again. The four of us drew up and dismounted, just after we'd passed Gembloux.

This time it was a slow puncture. Agnes unloaded Esme's machine and turned it upside down. 'You others had better watch what I do,' she suggested blithely. It seemed a good opportunity to show us the right way to mend one.

But we weren't very good students. Barbara, still sleepy, lay back against a wayside hump of grass and closed her eyes. Esme, whose bike it was and who therefore should have showed some interest, began to dab some ointment onto her delicate fair skin, which was already beginning to peel; a result of being out so long in the strong sunlight and fresh air.

I did start to watch, when suddenly my attention was caught by two young men, wearing haversacks, walking up the hill towards us. Esme, seeing them, left off dabbing her face to observe them better.

One was tall, bearded, very dark; the other blond – his fair skin had been so tanned by the sun that his eyebrows and hair looked even paler in contrast.

They soon caught sight of us and seeing Agnes – holding a spanner, with Esme's equipment scattered around her – stopped.

'You want any help?' the bearded one asked.

They spoke English. What a relief. Agnes, who had been concentrating too hard on the bike to notice their approach, looked up at them flushed. She was no mechanic, as we other three knew.

'My friend's bike is a new sort of model, which makes it rather complicated,' she explained, trying to justify her slowness. Then added, 'But it's only a puncture.'

'Too bad,' the bearded one took her place and examined the bike with quick competence.

'You English?' Agnes asked, delighted to be relieved of her task.

'Australian,' he replied laconically. 'Say, this hole's not too big. Shouldn't take long to fix it. I'm Pete and he's John.' He pointed to his friend, who was now squatting placidly by the roadside, clearly glad of an excuse to rest.

We others talked to him, leaving Pete to Agnes. The two young men seemed a wild pair compared to us. We discovered that they were travelling really rough, walking, but picking up lifts whenever they could. They seemed to sleep anywhere. Sometimes under bridges, or on park benches, behind haystacks or hedges, or maybe, if lucky, in a barn.

'We're hiking through Belgium, Luxembourg and France,' John said yawning. 'Then it's home.'

'We're making for Profondville tonight,' Agnes put in overhearing. 'We're hoping to get to Spain eventually.'

'*Spain*? On those things?' Both men looked at us suspiciously, as if we were pulling their legs.

'Well, you'll have to have a move on if you want to get to Profondville tonight,' Pete said. He'd finished mending Esme's bike, which was just as well. Not long after he'd straightened himself up, a large trailer lorry climbed the hill behind us. The two men hailed it. The driver obligingly stopped and allowed them both to scramble aboard.

'So long – have a good time, girls,' Pete shouted mockingly as the four of us started to pick up our encumbered bicycles.

'Perhaps we'll meet again – somewhere...' John grinned back at us. Their two waving figures disappeared from view.

So it was on once more. Before long, the road to Namur suddenly steepened and we found ourselves swooping down into this dusty, straggling, rather dull manufacturing town. In spite of the hold-up, we felt too hungry not to stop and eat a brief meal of bread and cheese in the park, near a waterfall. High above us loomed the grey rock of the town's fortress.

It was after Namur, situated at the junction of the Sambre and the Meuse and at the beginning of the Ardennes, that the picturesque part of our journey started. For now we were riding along the Meuse with its chugging steamers, lazy boats and swimmers. Although the cobblestoned road made us bump up and down, it was a pleasant and peaceful ride, past pink-and-white-shuttered houses, orchards and women selling strawberries beneath striped sunshades.

Alas, though, first dusk then darkness descended too quickly for us. However, the river did look particularly beautiful by moonlight. Tawny-tinted rocks rose sheer above the grey-pointed rooftops, while welcoming lights from the hotels and houses splashed across the water, daubing it with a variety of colours. Occasionally an illuminated shrine glowed eerily out at us from the shadows.

But we could see nowhere, absolutely nowhere round about where we could erect our tent.

Before we reached Profondville, Agnes stopped to ask a man where we could go. He directed us to a brown gabled house standing on grey bricks beside the river. It was called 'Les Amis de la Nature' and was a cheap hostel for 'plus âgés' – Belgians too old for ordinary hostels – and foreigners. Apparently there were many of these places in the Ardennes area. Behind it was a campsite. It wasn't long before our small brown tent took its place beside the other dim shapes.

5

HELPING A FELLOW COUNTRYMAN

The next part of our journey was a real scramble. Friday was the day we were due to arrive at Georges's home, and it was after eleven when we left the hostel.

Although we had breakfast in the communal dining room to save time, there was still the tent to take down and the baggage to pack. Everything that went into the panniers and baskets had to be tightly compressed. This meant a lot of pushing and squeezing. Then it all had to be strapped very tightly onto our bikes so that it wouldn't slip off.

'We'll never make it,' Agnes told us, exasperated. 'You'll just have to move your legs faster.' This had become a constant moan from her to us other three. She didn't think we were trying hard enough, especially Esme.

Also distances on maps often worked out longer than you thought when you were trying to cycle them. Fortunately for us, the road beside the river was fairly free of traffic. It was quiet, too. There were many men fishing peacefully from the banks.

We stopped for a brief rest at a bridge near Houx. This was an area containing three châteaux and some interesting grottos, but there was no time to explore. Then we made towards Dinant, a very old town, which had existed even before Roman times. It had been built on the route of so many marching armies that it was said to have been destroyed and rebuilt four hundred times. Today's town was a juxtaposition of styles. Medieval houses, modern ones, an onion-shaped dome church, tall steeples and, of course, the inevitable stern citadel, reached now by swinging yellow funicular chairs. It had become a peaceful, picturesque holiday centre. By now it was late afternoon. We ate some more food, then it was on again.

We rode up and down hills, through forests, leaving the river behind. But as hard as we struggled onwards, we knew in our hearts that we would not be able to reach Georges's home that day. Our loads were too heavy: we were not sufficiently practised cyclists. The large cobblestones we had encountered on some of the roads made us feel as if we were riding horses. The constant bumping up and down would cause a basket to break loose and skid dangerously across the road. Then the owner would have to wearily dismount, pick it up, and strap it back in place again, while the others impatiently waited.

That evening when darkness fell, the sky was heavy and overcast.

'I suppose we should try and find a campsite,' Agnes said at last. Even she, who had been so persistently optimistic that we might, if we really tried hard, reach Georges's house, realised that it was looking increasingly impossible.

'Couldn't we have a meal somewhere?' an exhausted Barbara suggested.

It was me who suddenly espied a squarish white building, the Café d'Or, not too prosperous-looking or expensive, but not too shabby either, down a side-turning off the main road. Friendly lights glowed from it across the street.

'*Bonjour mesdemoiselles.*' A plump round-faced woman, wearing the uniform black dress although she did not look particularly old, greeted us with a hospitable smile.

'*Oui, oui.*' She nodded her head vigorously when Agnes asked if we could get a cheap meal there.

Later, when she brought us a bowl of fresh lettuces and a dish of hot chips on a tray, Agnes – urged by us other three – asked if she knew of a cheap site nearby.

However, Agnes's French was too English for the woman to understand it unaided. She called 'Henri' twice through the kitchen doorway. He was her husband, a short, rather sullen-faced man. He quickly cut into Agnes's recitation with a few terse words.

Agnes translated this into what seemed a fairly long speech. 'He says we can use the orchard behind the house but we must finish our meal first. Also, he said that there is an anglais living in the village who will come and interpret for us.'

'He said all that!' I put in disbelieving.

However, it seemed that Agnes's interpretation was correct. But the proprietor didn't seem very happy about our camping.

He kept looking out of the window and shaking his head.

When the *anglais* had been fetched we had finished eating and had begun to erect our tent.

He was a tall, slim, large-featured man and spoke with a north country accent. To begin with he appeared rather abrupt.

'Henri doesn't want you to sleep in the orchard. He thinks it will rain, also the ground's too damp.' Then he added, more amiably: 'He likes *les femmes* and thinks you will be uncomfortable. He says you may sleep in the house for nothing.'

We were determined to explain to him, and to anyone else that we met, that we weren't scroungers. We had chosen to cycle and camp round Europe and that was what we intended to do. We assured him that our tent was waterproof and that we preferred to camp.

'All right, all right.' He held up one hand as if warding off blows. His manner changed. He suddenly became quite friendly.

'Look, my name's Murray. I don't often have the chance to speak to English people here. Come round to my house and meet my Belgian wife.'

The four of us refused politely.

'We have to get up very early tomorrow to get to my friend Georges's house, near Virton. It's still quite a distance away,' Agnes said.

Mr Murray looked disappointed. 'Well, come inside and have a drink with Henri and his wife. It won't take long. And it would help me. They say here that the English aren't friendly.'

Then, in spite of our protestations, the proprietor interrupted us and insisted that we sleep in the house. He was adamant.

Mr Murray said that if we slept in the house for nothing – even though we didn't really want to – we would have to have a drink with Henri and his wife out of courtesy.

'There seems nothing we can do about it,' I grumbled, sighing philosophically.' We were so tired. We replaced the tent in the bag and returned with him to the café.

Thankfully, we were only offered Belgian beer, although this proved potent enough. The proprietor's sullenness gradually diminished as he drank. He became convivial and called 'Chin chin', an English expression he knew, and insisted we drank up quickly so that he could refill our glasses.

Mr Murray whispered to us that we must do as he said. 'Otherwise he'll think that the English can't drink.' We obeyed, thinking naïvely that maybe the honour of our country was at stake. Agnes, who had the habit of waving her arms when she spoke, began to flail them like windmills, which fascinated Henri, our host.

'She is an amazon. They're all amazons. Such fine girls could be found nowhere else but in England,' Mr Murray translated. He was delighted with us.

'My prestige is mounting,' he whispered to me, adding: 'Believe me, it is not always easy being the only Englishman in the village.'

Suddenly, Henri leaned forward and shot a barrage of questions at us.

'He asks where are you going and what do you do? Also, are not Englishmen good enough for you that you have to come to Europe to find better men?'

Still exhausted from our long ride and half silly from the effects of the beer, we were only able to gaze at him dully. I saw the room blur into a sleepy mist. Agnes's arms were beginning to flail more lethargically, as windmill sails do when the wind drops. Even so, she stumbled to answer him in French.

'*Nous célébrons. Nous faisons le tour d'Europe à bicyclette...*' She tailed off, looking at Mr Murray for help. He was now standing up.

'You girls must come and have breakfast with me and my wife tomorrow. Come at eight-thirty, or nine... or whenever you like.'

Agnes took his cue: she started to rise. '*Nous couchons.*'

'Ah, *couchez*,' Henri, who had started to wrap Esme in one of the long window curtains, suddenly released her, so that she spun and fell – quite gracefully, considering – but giggling hysterically, onto the table.

The proprietor then beckoned the four of us to follow him, which we did, picking up our baggage on the way, as he led us upstairs to a room furnished with only a wash basin. We all felt a little tipsy, especially Barbara, as we stood meekly in its centre, awaiting his return, with two large mattresses which he bowled through the doorway.

'*Je regrette de ne pas avoir de lits,*' he told us regretfully. Then '*Au revoir,*' and he was gone.

It was not quite the end of the matter. Just as we were falling asleep in a tangle of sleeping bags and clothes, there was a short, sharp knock on the door. Barbara crawled over to open it. Henri's wife stood outside, smiling benignly down at us. She handed Barbara a large key, winked, then was gone.

6

BOUILLON

Of course, we overslept.

I was lying in a tight ball, with Esme stretched out beside me, when I heard Agnes shout despairingly.

'IT'S ELEVEN O'CLOCK!'

When I hastily unwound myself, Agnes was standing up, still wrapped in her long sleeping bag, her watch in one hand.

Poor Barbara, the only one out of her sleeping bag, was sitting on one of the mattresses, her face in her hands.

Naturally we other three felt sorry for her but knew she had to be galvanised, shaken, roused out of her misery. There was simply no time to lose. Within half an hour we were washed, dressed, packed and tumbling down the staircase. Oh, why had nobody called us?

We found the proprietor waiting downstairs in the café. Alas, the jolly, convivial Henri of last night had been replaced by his former, rather sullen self. He merely gave us a curt nod when we thanked him for letting us sleep in his house and said our goodbyes. His wife was nowhere to be seen.

Mrs Murray, a dark vivacious woman, did not seem at all put out by our late arrival. Maybe she had expected it. She spoke English well but impatiently, as if striving to find the right word for something irritated her.

Breakfast was still set in her living room. There were bread and rolls, butter, jam, slabs of chocolate and cups of delicious coffee, which she made afresh over the tiled stove.

'It's such a pity that Barbara has to miss this,' Agnes whispered to me as Barbara sat white-faced and miserable on the sofa, trying hard not to look at us eating, although she did eventually manage to sip a cup of black coffee.

Mrs Murray apologised for her husband's absence. 'He had to go to work. It's not often he gets the chance to speak to people from his own country,' she added regretfully.

We told her about our trip to date and our plans for later. In turn, she entertained us with stories about her life in Belgium. We found the most interesting the one about how she and her husband had met during the war.

She had always lived in the village; even during the invasion of her country, the German occupation and its liberation.

Towards the end of the war, when there had been much fighting going on in her neighbourhood, many villagers had moved away out of danger. But she had had to stay on, because her father, then alive, was very ill, and could not be moved.

'I was often very frightened by the noise made by the bombing and shelling. There was very little news about the progress of the war – only rumour. No one knew where the Germans and English and other allies were, or who was advancing, and who retreating.'

Then one morning she had looked out of the window and seen a tank rolling by. To her horror, it stopped by her gate. A steel-helmeted soldier clambered out. She was petrified. She did not know which army he belonged to.

'But it was a tommy.' She threw up her hands vivaciously. 'It was Mr Murray. And – typical English – he only wanted me to give him some fresh water so that he could brew tea. I was delighted. I had never felt so happy. Tea! I asked him in. I gave him food. I embraced him. My liberator!'

But the war had still been going on. So Mr Murray continued with the rest of the British army into Germany. She had written letters to him, helped by an old English dictionary. They were married about two years later.

'We lived in England to begin with, but I hated it because I found Newcastle cold and wet, and the people, too. Brrh!' she shuddered. So she had persuaded him to return to Belgium with her. Now he worked in a nearby factory. But alas, we never saw him again.

We did not leave the Murrays' home until about twelve-thirty, by which time Barbara had sufficiently recovered to allow us to resume our journey. In fact, it was she who suggested we try and reach Bouillon, where Mrs Murray had told us there was a hostel. It was now Saturday. Even Agnes realised it would be quite impossible for us to reach Georges's home that day.

As predicted by Henri, there had been much rain in the night and early morning. The sky was filled with dark clouds. We had not been long on the road when the light drizzle still falling became heavier. We were obliged to dismount and put on our translucent plastic capes and sou'wester hats, especially bought for this trip. We splashed on through straggling, untidy villages and dripping forests, resembling a small army of white ghosts.

When we finally sped down the steep road into Bouillon, the rain was falling so hard that we had to seek shelter for a while in a half-built house.

'*Montez, montez!*' Some young boys, playing dangerously amongst the paint pots and ladders, left off their games to point up the hill when Agnes asked for the *auberge de jeunesse*.

'Oh, why do they always have to put hostels on a hill?' Barbara grumbled as the four of us pushed our bikes over the cobblestones to the red-shuttered, buff-coloured building at the top.

By now, we were drenched and spattered with mud. The 'Father' (the warden at a hostel was always referred to as 'Father' or 'Mother') had to shut the door quickly after us to keep out the driving force of the wind and rain. He was a good-natured, kindly man and was not too put out by our capes dripping dirty puddles all over the clean floor; neither by the fact that we hadn't booked and had arrived late.

The dining room was already crowded with people when we entered. The hostellers had just finished their evening meal and were about to launch into a sing-song. The Father, who spoke English but with a strong German accent, brought us some food – salad, bread and tea – which he explained regretfully was all that was left. He had a round, jolly face, owlish spectacles and very short, spiky hair. For some reason, he put me in mind of a character out of Dickens' *Pickwick Papers*. He kept winking at us, especially at Esme and me, the youngest. We probably looked particularly miserable and wet. Barbara had completely recovered and Agnes was never put down for long.

While we were hungrily eating, he handed out some song-books to the other hostellers. Quite soon their cheerful, carolling voices seemed to ebb and flow like a gigantic sea all around us.

We four were embarrassed by this as we felt we were being sung to. This feeling was increased when the hostellers sang 'My Bonny lies over the Ocean', we believed in our honour. However, worse was yet to come. When it was seen that we had finished eating, someone called out, 'Now you English – a song please.'

To Barbara's, Agnes's and my surprise – and gratitude – it was Esme who came to the rescue. She had once apparently had private singing lessons. She had a melodious if not very strong voice and sang 'Rose of Tralee'.

When she had finished, the applause was thunderous, especially from the men, who stamped their feet and clapped their hands, shouting, 'Encore! Encore! More! More!' Their clamour died down when the Father stepped forward, unexpectedly authoritative, and held up one hand.

He seemed to give a signal – a sort of barked command. A few of the hostellers swiftly collected up the song-books. The rest of them obediently lined up outside his room. They had to obtain sleeping bags from him before going to bed.

'What a good thing we've got ours. Those orange parachute ones will save us some money,' Agnes said.

To make sure that we would be allowed to use them, we pushed Esme forward holding one, hoping that we'd be able to cash in on her singing success. It looked a bit odd – rather gaudy and crumpled – when she held it up hopefully beside the newly-laundered white ones the other hostellers were now holding.

However, the friendly Father looked at it, then at her, winked 'Ja, ja' and passed her on swiftly.

Yet trouble still lay ahead.

It was me, unlucky me, who encountered it. Somehow I had accidentally contrived to be first in the queue outside the girls' locked dormitory.

Now this hostel possessed a Mother as well as a Father. This particular one was a gaunt, grim-looking woman, who wore her greying hair drawn back in a wispy bun. The long queue of impatient girls behind me seemed to make her hot and flustered. Also belligerent. Her self-appointed job was to stand guard to see that each girl admitted held a proper sleeping-bag.

I held up my bright orange one, trying to ignore the titters behind me.

'Vot is dat?' she asked scornfully, feeling the nylon material.

'The Father passed it,' I answered, but without much confidence.

'Impossible! Impossible!' she scolded me indignantly. Then, tearing it from my grasp, unlocked the door and measured it against the nearest bed.

'Komm!' Without waiting for any more explanations, she grabbed me by the arm and almost pulled me down to the kitchen where the Father now was. There followed a fierce argument in German, which I could not follow. The Mother shouted at the Father and the Father shouted back at the Mother, although every now and again he turned and winked at me as if to say it was not anything like as serious as it sounded. Finally they both measured me, the sleeping bag and, rather unexpectedly, the table.

'IMPOSSIBLE! IMPOSSIBLE!' shouted the Mother.

Fortunately for us, the Father got his way in the end, although there was a compromise of sorts. At his suggestion, we placed our butter-muslin towels over the pillows, which our sleeping bags were not quite long enough to cover.

Our victory, if you could call it that, caused a certain amount of comment and possibly some jealousy from the other girls who had watched the first part of the performance and probably heard the last.

'The Father kisses us all goodnight and brings us tea in bed in the morning,' a blonde girl – whom I had previously had difficulty making understand that I wanted her to move her case – suddenly called down from the bunk above in perfect English. She and the other girls appeared to resent what seemed to be the Father's favouritism towards us four.

I ignored this remark, not wanting to make any more trouble, but the conversation that followed in Dutch and German between her and other inmates I was sure was about us. We felt very conspicuous in our bright orange wrappings and wished we were sleeping in our tent, small though it was. We felt relieved when the Mother finally entered to see that everything was in order for the night.

The hostel was not unlike an institution. The Mother solemnly opened the windows a few inches – enough to let in the air but not wide enough to allow anyone to climb in or out. Then before she locked the door noisily behind her, she walked over to me, glaring as if expecting some new treason.

'It is forbidden to rise before seven.' Such a warning seemed the height of absurdity, especially to us. Agnes, Barbara, Esme and I exploded with laughter into the secrecy of our bedclothes.

7

AN UNEXPECTED SETBACK

It was about seven-thirty when we got up the following morning. The dormitory door was unlocked: there was a great flurry and scurry of girls rushing about with wash-bags and towels. The room was locked again at eight o'clock sharp. Woe betide anyone still found in bed, or undressed, or even just inside the room.

The four of us decided that this was probably a good thing. It meant we could make a really early start and perhaps get to Georges's house about lunch-time. Today was Sunday.

'We'll just have time to see him before he returns to Brussels,' Agnes said.

Alas for our plans. It seemed that the Mother had neither forgotten nor forgiven last night's victory. She still had her eyes on us and had determined that we be punished for our non-conformity.

After breakfast, when a smiling Agnes walked over to the bureau to collect our Youth Hostel Association cards, she refused to give them up.

Instead, very sharply: 'What room are you in?' As if she didn't know.

'Number two,' Agnes answered, surprised.

'Then you will first fold the blankets and sweep the floor. Another of you can sweep the floor in the dining room – also wipe down the tables. Then there are the toilets, the baths and wash-basins, also the kitchen...'

More than two hours later we were still busy at these tasks and we may well have been given more duties had not the Father, who had been out before, returned and intervened.

He was still winking at us, although now perhaps ruefully, almost apologetically, when the four of us finally departed on our way.

Bouillon – whose houses are a blend of French and German styles – climbs steeply from the valley, either side of the weedy green Semois, and is one of Belgium's most attractive towns. Its castle is magnificent and one of the best of its kind in Europe. Godefroy de Bouillon was supposed to have led the first Crusade from this stronghold, which was also used by the American military during the Second World War. We paused to look awhile.

'We'll just have to come back one day,' I said regretfully as we finally sped off.

That day's journey took us into the heart of the Ardennes, through undulating forests. We rode between trees and ferns, past bubbling streams and carpets of flowers. Along one side of us lay France. Almost every signpost seemed to point to the venue of a famous battlefield, either of the last war, or the one before that. The Germans had advanced over the nearby River Meuse and into this part of Belgium before going on into France, thus skirting the supposed impregnable Maginot Line.

We ate our lunch in the forest, in the shade of tall pines and spruce. While exploring on an errand to get water for our pan from a quick-flowing brook, I unearthed a rusty helmet. It was a ghoulish reminder that we were probably dining in one of the most bloodstained corners of Europe.

It was eerily quiet. The tall, straight trees might have been lines of watching, green-coated soldiers, patiently awaiting the axe. It was chilling to think how many men must have died around where we sat in the woods.

By the time we reached Florenville, it was late afternoon. Agnes, still optimistic, hadn't entirely lost hope that we might see Georges again. She decided to try and phone him from a café. Barbara, Esme and I, listening, heard a few minutes of agitated speech. Then she emerged sorrowfully from the phone booth, telling us – we'd already guessed – that we were too late.

'He's returning to Brussels. He's just left for the station.'

Even so, the valiant Agnes decided to ride on ahead of us three to the railway line so that she could watch his train go by.

But before she, or we others close behind, reached the level-crossing gate, the train to Brussels flashed past. We were too far off and the train was going too fast for us to have much more than a very brief glimpse of what might have been Georges waving from the last carriage but one.

8

GEORGES'S HOME

Not only had Georges gone by the time we arrived at his home, but his parents were out, too, for lunch. In Belgium, like France, these occasions are often gargantuan feasts with sometimes as many as 14 courses, and can last for hours.

Their home was easy to find. It was a tall, white, rambling building, set alongside a rushing stream on the main road, about half a kilometre from the last house in the village. We were expected, though: our arrival was awaited by relatives, Georges's mother's sister and her husband.

We dismounted, lying our bikes by the roadside – there was no fence – and walked to the front door. It was swung open before we had a chance to knock.

'So, here they are – at last!' Georges's aunt, a tall, angular, dark-haired woman, looked down on us scornfully, her arms folded.

'We've arrived!' Agnes said, rather unnecessarily, giving her usual beaming smile. She was disappointed about our having missed Georges, but not unduly so. To reach here within the stipulated time had been a challenge to her ingenuity and leadership. That she had failed was not really her fault. It had been a combination of bad luck, troublesome bikes and weak-legged friends.

'And where are you going to sleep?' the lady asked bluntly, rather as if she suspected we might have designs on her bed.

'We have a tent,' Agnes explained, but less exuberantly. 'We can pitch it in the field over there.' She ran her eyes professionally over a stretch of land beyond the wide untidy garden.

'I think you all need your brains testin',' Georges's aunt told us tartly. 'The ground's soppin' and it's bitin' cold.' She shivered, drawing her coat, which apparently she even wore indoors, more firmly round her.

'Aye, they're barmy.' Mr Baker, her husband – a hefty man, about fifty-five and sporting a black beret – came into view, sucking at his pipe.

They didn't intend to be rude. It was just their style. They believed in being straightforward, speaking their minds, and never, never giving anything but the most grudging praise.

However, they showed themselves to be good-hearted underneath, for after a few sucks at his pipe, Mr Baker suddenly said, 'They can use the orchard. It's a nice spot and they'll be out of the way.'

Then Mrs Baker softened and asked if we were hungry.

We nodded. As usual, we were famished.

'My sister won't be back until about nine,' she continued. 'They stuff themselves like pigs in this country. I'll find you something in the pantry.'

Mr Baker thought we should put up our tent before we ate. We followed him into the orchard, climbing a flight of grassy steps. It was rather like going upstairs to a bedroom. We finally chose a wide plateau, surrounded by apple, pear and cherry trees, which formed a sort of protective leafy wall around us.

Mr Baker thawed considerably as he helped us erect the tent and even suggested he take us on a tour of the village after we'd eaten his wife's meal.

He proved to be a very good guide. He loved Belgium, especially this part, and had often stayed here before with his wife. He would have liked to live here. As this wasn't possible he had to content himself with occasional visits, wearing a black beret and using '*Oui, oui*' and '*Merci*' a lot in his conversation. He also said '*Bonsoir*' to everyone we passed in the roadway.

The village, only a few metres from France, was very old. The lime tree standing in its centre had been used as a meeting place for the elders for hundreds of years. Some of the surrounding cottages, small and dirty, had pear trees growing flatly up their grey stone walls. There were stacks of wood, heaps of manure and straw standing beside many of the doorways, as if they were all part of a large and messy farmyard.

We had noticed previously while cycling through the Ardennes region how poor and shabby many of the villages were, with dirty cobbled streets and often cavelike houses. Mr Baker told us it was because it was Walloon, French-speaking country. The people living here, he said, tended to be more happy-go-lucky and less bothered about appearances than the tidier, Dutch-like Flemings in the North and West. Also, they'd been overrun and occupied so many times they didn't trust their rulers, and never advertised the fact that they might have any money.

'But they're probably not as badly off as you think,' Mr Baker said. 'They don't use banks much. They'd rather hide their money under floorboards or behind fireplaces. Each house is self-supporting. The occupant has his own piece of land, his cow, his chickens. They till their fields communally, using a jeep to pull their motorless tractor.'

We also learned that the village owned the surrounding woodland, which was arranged in thirty plots.

'It takes about thirty years to grow a tree. When they cut down one plot, they always plant another,' Mr Baker told us. Georges's mother had had a plot planted for her son when he was born, but this, like others, had been cut down and burned by the German occupying army.

Mr Baker also pointed out that white elephant, the Maginot Line, on the horizon.

'It cost the French millions of francs to build but the Germans invaded through unprotected Belgium, who weren't then in the war, and eventually surrounded it.' It was now unused, pointless and falling into disrepair.

Suddenly, as we four were gazing up into the wooded hills, a large car drew up, brakes screeching, startling us and making us jump sharply to one side.

'Hello Tom, Agnes and the three cycling friends,' Georges's mother shouted in a cracked, excited voice, smiling at us. 'I hope you girls are not too tired after your long ride.'

The lift she gave us back to her house was somewhat erratic as she was still merry from the effects of the luncheon. However, she assured us that she was a very safe driver. 'I've not had many accidents. Only knocked down two cats and a dog – oh, and a goose. Not bad for thirty years of driving, eh?'

When we were all back safely at the house, we were expected to celebrate our journey and safe arrival with Madame du Bois. She gave us a glass each of her special home-made cherry brandy, which we drank together in her long sitting room. It stretched the length of the house and overlooked the stream. A passageway had been built across this, thus joining the house to Monsieur du Bois's office and sawmill on the other side.

The sitting room seemed to be crammed with rather elegant but not very comfortable French furniture, also lots of knick-knacks, potted plants and big vases. Two large glass-fronted cabinets exhibited Madame du Bois's collection of Flemish dolls and tiny cups, saucers and plates. A big stove, unlit, stood in one corner of the room.

Madame du Bois, small, lively and vivacious, was in striking contrast to her rather dour sister. She laughed and chatted continuously as she moved quickly round the room, filling glasses and pulling out tables and chairs.

'How long are you going to stay?' she asked. 'Perhaps a week. Then you'll see Georges when he comes next weekend.'

We told her regretfully that this would not be possible.

'We've only got a short amount of time and we've still six more countries to visit,' Agnes added.

'Six more countries!' Madame du Bois exclaimed in horror. 'And on bicycles. What a task!'

But before Mr Baker had time to put in, 'They're barmy,' Agnes wisely changed the subject. She said that her friend, Georges's cousin, had asked her to send the family her love if we managed to call during our journey.

'We've not met for years.' Madame du Bois sat down. 'Let me see. I went over to England last in 1939 – just before the war. Georges was still a child.'

'Were you here during the German occupation?' I asked. We were all very curious to know what it had been like.

'Oh, yes,' she answered gaily, then added: 'We are on the main road to Arlon. So all the armies came past this house. The French were the first when the Germans invaded Belgium. They soon returned when they were forced to retreat. People from here were evacuated to the south of France just before the German soldiers arrived here. But we came back after three months.

'Oh, what a state the house was in. Furniture broken, empty bottles everywhere. Many things had been stolen.' She sipped her brandy thoughtfully as she cast her mind back to those days.

'My husband was the Burgomaster – that is, the mayor – here. The Germans respected his position but they often took him round with them, especially if they thought they might be ambushed. People hid in the forests to escape the Germans all through the war. You can imagine how afraid I was for his life.

'He played along with the Germans, pretending to be friendly while I organised the local resistance movement. The Germans did not know I was English. No one in the village told on me. Because of my husband's position, I had good connections with the police, who were mostly patriots here – not like in France. They used to get me ration cards, also an official stamp. I forged signatures on the cards and stamped them to give to people on the run.'

It seemed that she'd hidden many fugitives in the rambling old house, such as a Jewish woman whose husband hid in the nearby monastery, and two RAF pilots who had been shot down.

'Were you ever in danger of being caught?' Barbara asked.

'All the time there was danger!' Madame du Bois put a thin hand over her heart.

'One day I made a ration card for a young Algerian. Then he went off in a lorry with some fellows. They all carried guns. It was defiance, a silly trick. The Germans stopped them, then found their guns and shot them. The Algerian could have told about me and perhaps have saved his own life.

'Another time I sent a young man to Liège to our headquarters there to get money in exchange for ration cards. I had plenty of ration cards but no money. He was found in the train by the Germans, tortured and sent to Buchenwald. He never spoke. After that, I sent Georges to Liège to get money. I did not think they would suspect a young schoolboy.

'Then there was the time the Germans came into the house. They were laughing and talking in the kitchen while I was here in this room with all the cards and the rubber stamp I used. I did not have time to put them away.'

'You must have been very glad when the war was over,' Barbara put in.

'Glad! Oh, yes.' She raised her eyebrows expressively. 'When the Americans arrived here with their tanks, they knocked down part of this house. Even so, we were glad to see them. The Germans had intended to stay and fight here. They even set up a gun in the place where your tent is now well camouflaged by the trees. Fortunately for everyone, they changed their minds and went away.

'Oh, what a time it was,' she continued, remembering. 'There were Germans escaping to Germany, Americans and Britons advancing, prisoners escaping from their prison camps. I took in and hid two starving Russians who ate like wild animals. They were afraid of being shot by everyone.

'So, you see, this village has not always been as peaceful as it is now. I have fed soldiers of all nationalities – Americans, Canadians, Welsh, French – and given them wine in my kitchen.'

'You must be a great sport!' Barbara told her.

'You were lucky to have such experiences. It gives you something to talk about,' Mrs Baker put in tartly. Although she was probably proud of her sister's exploits, she dared not allow her to become swollen-headed.

'Lucky!' Madame du Bois almost exploded.

'Aye,' Mr Baker nodded, agreeing with his wife.

Perhaps it was just as well that Georges's father, still flushed and merry from the luncheon, chose that moment to arrive home.

Monsieur du Bois was in high spirits. After another cherry brandy to celebrate our safe arrival, he and Mr Baker, both carrying hurricane lamps, and with many guffaws and jokes, escorted the four of us to our orchard bedroom.

We stayed one day longer than we had intended at Georges's home. The following morning when we were awakened unexpectedly by Mr Baker bringing each of us a mug of tea on a tray, he told us that his sister-in-law had suggested we do our washing and leave tomorrow instead of today.

Needless to say, we didn't need much persuasion. Our clothes were already filthy. And a day of rest from cycling was very welcome. It would also give us the opportunity to write some cards.

Madame du Bois, like most people, had no washing machine. There wasn't a lot of room in her kitchen for all four of us together. Even so, we managed quite well by using a tub of hot water in the garage. After a good soaping, we rinsed our clothes in the stream that flowed past the house.

Our chief difficulty was that the water was so fast that we had to hold on tightly to our belongings to prevent them from being swept away. I lost a hanky and Esme a sock, which like all the floating debris and household waste probably ended up in France.

Luxembourg was our next day's destination. The du Bois and Bakers saw us off.

'Send us a postcard. Let us know how you get on,' our hostess shouted after us.

'*Bon voyage!*' Mr Baker called in his gruff voice. 'Let us know when you get home.'

Although he and his wife had stopped calling us 'barmy' and 'daft', neither of them, or even the du Bois, really thought we would get very far.

9

LUXEMBOURG

This, our first visit to Luxembourg, was a particularly happy one. There was a pleasant surprise awaiting us there.

Luxembourg City is picturesque in a military way, in that it resembles a great sprawling castle. Indeed, until it was dismantled in 1867, it was reckoned to be one of the strongest fortresses in the world.

It is built on two levels around the Bock, a mighty mass of rock, honeycombed with passages. The upper part of the city is connected with the lower by steps, winding roads and viaducts. Towers, walls, ruins and rocks seem to stick haphazardly out of the ground wherever one looks.

It took us the best part of a day to reach the city. Our ride had taken us through flattish, rather dull countryside, passing many rows of small dowdy houses, cultivated fields and orchards. The frontier into the country of Luxembourg had been rather a disappointment: merely one guard sitting in a wooden shelter, eating sandwiches out of a paper bag. He scarcely bothered to glance at us as we self-consciously pushed our bikes past his post.

It was early evening when we actually arrived at Luxembourg City. By then, it was too late to start looking for a campsite. We had discovered by looking at a map we got at the railway station information office that there should be a hostel somewhere in the centre. That's if this mazelike, upside down sort of place could be said to have a centre. We bumped over tramlines up the Avenue de la Liberté and took the third turning on the left after the flag-draped Pont Adolphe, which led to the Place d'Armes. Here, the street narrowed.

Agnes had spread the flimsy blue map over her handlebars so that she could look up and read the street names on their blue plates, set up high on the tall houses. We finally stopped when we reached a bridge. According to our map, it looked as though the hostel should be somewhere at the bottom of the viaduct.

But how did we get to it? Long, grey, barrack-like houses, which might have been carved out of the rocky cliff itself, and high steeples appeared through the foliage. Great trees reached almost to the top of our bridge. Although a road twisted down to the valley like the letter 'S', it was difficult to see whether it would lead us to the hostel. We were tired and didn't want to make an unnecessary journey with our heavily-laden machines.

It was Esme who first saw them. Agnes, Barbara and I had dismounted to peer down into the leafy panorama, leaving Esme, who said she was too tired to move, guarding our bikes. We suddenly heard her shout, 'Look!'

When the three of us turned quickly, we were amazed to see our two Australian friends met in Belgium strolling along the centre of the roadway. But this time they were free of their haversacks. John's face was redder than it had been before and Pete's was even more hidden beneath the black bush of hairy growth.

Pete casually lifted one dark, fuzzy arm in recognition.

'Hi, there!' White teeth gleamed through the tangled beard. 'So you made it, girls.'

'Fancy us meeting again! What a coincidence!' Agnes exclaimed. Actually, it wasn't such a coincidence, really, for they had said they were going to Luxembourg. It turned out they had only arrived there the day before us.

As luck would have it, they knew exactly where the hostel was because they were staying there themselves. We only had to follow them – over the bridge and down the curling road to turn left at the bottom. Before long, we were all within the hostel gates in a courtyard, along with other groups of young men and women.

John advised us to register immediately as this hostel was popular and soon filled up. So we did, then had a good wash and tidy-up.

Most fortuitously, it seemed, we were able to put on our newly-washed dresses. It was rather as if yesterday's laundering had been in preparation for this event. Pete and John had offered to take us out to see the city and have a celebration meal. Was this to celebrate the fact that we had managed to arrive safely, or that we'd met up again? It was probably both.

Thus, two hours later, the four of us strolled through the gates again with the two men. Pete and John and Agnes and Barbara walked in front, while a rather weary Esme and I trailed some way behind.

Now that it was late evening there seemed to be an exhilarating magic in the atmosphere. The rugged cliffs, ruins and towers, although sternly grim, exuded a gruesome romance all their own. I imagined epic battles being fought in the squares with horses charging and swords flashing: or perhaps, more subtly, a sudden ambush and the sliding secrecy of an assassin's knife. There were so many creepy, cobblestoned corners, lanterns illuminating tiny courtyards and shadowy arches. And beside them lay the ravine, aglow with a myriad points of light.

None of us noticed much what we ate in the frugal café. We were all equally poor.

Agnes and Pete seemed to get on particularly well, perhaps because they were kindred spirits. Like her, he was in love with nature – the countryside, insects, birds and trees. She told us later, back in the hostel, that he'd been a schoolmaster in Australia, but had come to England to marry an English girl he'd met on holiday in Sydney. By the time he'd arrived, however, she'd found someone else. Disappointed and not keen to return home straight away, he was temporarily roaming round Europe with John, a friend he'd made in England. John had just finished an architectural course but thought he'd like to travel a bit before settling down.

As the hostel doors were locked for the night at ten, we couldn't stay out for long. It was not unusual for people to be locked out for the night, even if they were only a few minutes late.

Pete and John were leaving Luxembourg early the following morning: they were hoping to get a lift.

'We've done so well with lifts up to now, we might eventually go on to Spain,' John told Barbara. Like Pete and Agnes, the two of them seemed to have taken to one another.

PART TWO

10

AN UNCERTAIN RECEPTION

'Why don't you girls ditch those things?' Pete nodded towards the four bikes standing in the shed the next morning. 'You should hitch like us. You four would do well. You'll never get round Europe on those contraptions,' he added.

'Oh yes we will,' Agnes replied, nettled.

'I bet we get to Spain before you,' Barbara challenged.

'You'll need some luck!' John threw back his head, laughing.

Then it was, 'So long,' and 'Don't get too tired,' and they were off, disappearing out of our lives again.

We four left the hostel a few hours later. However, before finally leaving Luxembourg, we decided to explore the town by daylight and visit the casemates – galleries hewn out of the surrounding rocky cliffs – in which people had hidden during times of siege. They had also been occupied by troops.

According to the guidebook I bought, Luxembourg's recorded history began in 963 when Siegfried, Count of the Ardennes, had taken possession of the castle which stood on the Bock, looking down on the Alzette and Petrusse rivers. It was called Lucilinburhuc (small fortress) which later gave its name to the town and state.

But according to legend, Siegfried married the fairy Melusine, who was half mermaid. When he discovered her secret, she sank back into the rock – a punishment for her earthly marriage. Nevertheless, she apparently returns every seven years with a golden key in her mouth. Whoever takes this key may set her free and claim her as his bride. During her long imprisonment she works on a chemise of fine linen, adding one stitch to it every seven years. It is said that if her chemise is finished before she is freed, the fortress and the Bock will vanish into the earth.

Like Belgium, little Luxembourg has suffered many foreign rulers. She was occupied by the Germans during the two world wars. Even so, she has managed to retain a spirit of independence; her own language, a patois perhaps (a blend of German and French). She was neutralised and her independence guaranteed in 1867, when not only was her fortress dismantled but most of the passageways were also demolished.

Nevertheless, there was still enough there for us to visit. We descended into the dim interior, enclosed by thick rock walls. From the loopholes and look-out posts, where cannons had once been hidden, were marvellous views of the winding roads, parks, gardens and the buildings below.

By the time we left Luxembourg and were riding northwards towards Echternach, it was quite hot. Although this was a real improvement on the rain we had previously encountered, it was difficult for us to get up much speed.

Esme, in particular, was having an especially hard time. She rode at the back of our line of cycles and had to make a great effort to keep up, even with Barbara, who was also rather slow. I don't suppose the poor girl had ever had to work so hard in her life before. Agnes worried about her. I suppose she was wondering how Esme would be able to manage the rest of the tour if she found it so difficult to keep up now. Finally she rode back and cycled alongside her.

'Esme, your legs are hardly moving at all,' we heard her say chidingly, although trying to make her voice sound tactful.

'I'm pushing them as hard as I can.' Esme sounded as if she was almost in tears.

Agnes sighed and rode on back to the lead. But later, when we had cycled into Echternach, she stopped, took Esme's bike away from her and tried it herself. She cycled slowly, very slowly, round the three of us.

'It is the bike!' she exclaimed triumphantly. 'I thought it must be. I can hardly make it move.'

We were all glad that Esme had been exonerated. But what could be done now? It was too late to get it mended anywhere. It was already evening. The streets were deserted and the shops shuttered for the night.

Nobody then would have guessed that Echternach was to become a well-known tourist resort. There had been some fierce fighting in the area, the effects of which were still to be seen in the battered, bullet-marked walls of some houses, the occasional wrecked buildings and the general air of dilapidation.

'We'll have to camp somewhere,' Barbara remarked. Like Esme, she didn't feel she could keep going for much longer.

We looked around us. A bridge lay ahead, a barrier blocking its entrance. A soldier sat in a tall wooden hut beside it.

'You realise we've reached the frontier,' she added, exasperated.

'Let's go on into Germany,' I suggested. Although very tired, I still felt adventurous. And after all, we might just as well. We could pitch our tent on the other side of the Eure river, then look for a garage to mend Esme's bike the following day.

In any case, what else could we do? The only alternative was to cycle back into the town. The countryside we had passed through previously had looked built-up and cultivated. Ahead, beyond the bridge, loomed what looked like a wide stretch of uncultivated land.

'Perhaps we'd better use up the remains of our Luxembourg money. It's not supposed to be much use anywhere else,' I suggested.

'There must be a shop somewhere,' Agnes added, gazing round.

There was. But only a small one, and which only sold sweets, a few yards away from the frontier.

When I emptied the contents of the secret purse onto the counter, a white-haired old lady, aided by her granddaughter, helped us choose some sweets. She was a friendly soul and asked where we were going.

'To Germany. We have a tent,' Agnes explained in French, pointing through the window across the river.

To Germany! At once the old lady's face changed and her eyes enlarged with horror.

It was not safe. It was certainly not safe for four girls with a tent, she kept trying to tell us.

She was still standing beside her shop, shaking her head and watching, when we approached the frontier hut. The soldier inside also disapproved of our crossing the bridge at this hour. However, our passports were in order. He couldn't stop us. He shrugged as he swung up the barrier to let us through onto the bridge.

'Stay in Luxembourg. Germany is dangerous,' he shouted after us in English.

'Why do you want to visit the stinking Germans?' a boy on a bike called out to us as he suddenly sped through the quiet street behind.

We felt nervous, but having started to cross, we felt we had to go on. The sun was now sinking down behind the opposite hills and staining the river in front a deep blood red.

When we reached the end of the bridge we were confronted by two green-uniformed officials, who stared at us suspiciously. Why were we coming to Germany?

'*Touristes. Nous avons une tente.*' Agnes hopefully tried her friendly smile.

But this didn't work. It seemed they could not, or would not, understand her French. Barbara, who had learned German at school and who was to be our interpreter here, had to dig down into her bike's panniers and find our blue international phrase book. With its aid, she explained in stumbling German.

'Campers.' One official glanced disparagingly at our shabby baggage and scribbled chalk crosses over it. Perhaps four girls with heavily-loaded bikes were too unusual to be let through without some explanation. Then he waved us on.

At last we were in Germany.

Although still exhausted by our long ride, the warnings and unfriendly reception made us decide to put as much distance as we could between ourselves and the frontier.

By now, it was almost dark. The road seemed to wind in a zigzag fashion up the hill, reducing its steepness, but doubling the distance we had to ride. We could see no people about; no houses where we could ask permission to camp. There seemed to be nothing but hills and hedges, an occasional wide stretch of corn or field of hay, but no suitable place to pitch a tent.

It was eerily silent except for the call of night birds, including the cry of an owl as it swooped on its prey. We rode on and on.

11

THE MOSELLE VALLEY

It seemed a long time before we reached the summit of the hill and the road curved down into a village. At first, like Echternach, it appeared rundown and deserted. Then we noticed a shabbily-dressed girl standing on the pavement.

As we approached hopefully, Barbara worked out a sentence asking her if she knew where we could camp. The words emerged slowly while she fixed the girl with her gaze, as though trying to compel her to understand.

The girl stared back, tittered and looked as if she'd like to run away. Then, probably because she was curious, she changed her mind and beckoned us to follow her through the village.

The four of us felt extremely apprehensive as we wheeled our machines through the quiet, badly-lit streets. After all, the war had not been over long and we were in ex-enemy territory. Apart from the general dislike the Germans had obviously aroused in the countries through which we'd just passed, we all knew people or had had relatives and friends killed fighting them. And had not Barbara and I lost our first home in the bombing of London? Our feelings about the Germans were very mixed.

The village was small so the girl took us quickly to her house. Her mother appeared quite friendly although was naturally surprised to see us. She gently scolded her daughter for giggling after she had repeated our request.

After some thought, she led us down to the end of the street through a gap between houses and into a sloping field.

Although the ground was very hard and stony, with tufts of grass growing between the ridges, we decided that it would have to do. But erecting the tent here when exhausted was difficult.

Agnes took off one of her heavy walking shoes and began to knock the pegs in with it, while I followed suit, grumbling and groaning.

Then, to make matters worse, we had the uncomfortable feeling that we were being slowly surrounded. Figures, at first shadowy in the gathering darkness, began to encircle us. By now, we were really scared, especially after all the warnings we had had about Germany.

Unexpectedly, a voice spoke out of the gloom.

'Do you wish for a hammer?'

A thickset man, dressed in oil-stained dungarees, pushed his way through the crowd which had now collected round us, and waved one aloft. There was an encouraging murmur from the watching figures.

Agnes took it from him gratefully. But her excitement was such that when she aimed it a peg, she hit her hand instead.

'Permit us to help.' The man sounded sympathetic. The ice was broken! Quite soon, with many of the villagers helping, a rather lop-sided tent was erected.

It was about twelve when we finally settled down inside to sleep. The excitement and fear had made me ill and I had to crawl outside the tent and be sick. Then a thunderstorm broke overhead. The noise it made sounded like guns shaking our tent. The rain that followed beat down so hard against its thin material that Agnes and Barbara had to climb outside and put up the flysheet which we had forgotten to do in the confusion of so many people helping us put up the tent.

It was still wet when we awoke the following morning. Long pools of water lay between the ridges and glittering raindrops encrusted the tufts of grass. Thankfully, this meant we had no visitors. Esme dawdled over her toilette; Barbara, now our German interpreter, was able to work out some useful sentences with her small German dictionary; while I concentrated my attention on our finances now that we were to be working in another currency. Agnes spread out the map and began to work out our route in more detail.

It so happened that a member of Federal Union, which employed her, lived in Heidelberg, quite some distance away.

'We could probably reach the Moselle today,' she said, considering. 'Then we'll cross this mountain. Goodness knows how! It'll be a terrible climb. Then we'll make for the Rhine. Heidelberg's on the Neckar, further south.'

All this sounded fine – in theory.

Luckily, that morning's rain was only light and eventually eased off. A watery-looking sun squeezed itself between the clouds. Luckily for us, too, most of the villagers were at work. But the man who'd lent Agnes the hammer last night must have had some time to spare for he strolled over to us to talk. We discovered that he had been a prisoner-of-war in Lincolnshire and was glad of the chance to practise his English on us.

Also, and this was a real bonus, he was a mechanic by trade. To Esme's delight, he offered to mend her bike for her. She had been very depressed and even confessed to me that she could not bear the thought of having to leave the tour because of her faulty bike and face her parents at home as a failure. Yet, she said, 'I can't possibly ride this bike for another day, then try and wheel it over a mountain.'

'Easy for me to fix.' The fellow grinned at her cheerfully.

'Not easy for me,' she told him ruefully.

'No,' he agreed, then added firmly: 'Not good for girls to travel through Germany without men.'

He set to work speedily and competently. He didn't seem to bear any malice against us for his having been a prisoner-of-war in our country. In fact, he talked quite nostalgically about his stay in England, as if he'd enjoyed it. Almost a holiday, he said, away from the fighting. Quite a number of German prisoners had worked on English farms during the war. They were usually fairer than the average Englishman and could also be recognised as prisoners by the coloured patches they were obliged to wear on their overalls.

We had more visitors after he'd finished mending Esme's bike and returned to his garage. This time they were children on their way home from school. It was about noon by now and they were going home for lunch. They must have been in bed when we arrived the previous night. No doubt they were surprised to see a small brown tent in the centre of a field in which they probably played.

They were neat and clean but rather thin. At first, they seemed shy and cautious, looking at us curiously, then pretending to play a game as they edged nearer to, then examined, the four bikes stacked beneath a tree.

They were also quite mischievous. After whispering and giggling together, they ran off, but returned shortly afterwards accompanied by a stout white pig, which they drove almost up to our tent doorway.

We had hoped to leave as soon as we'd packed our equipment. But after making friends with the children – and the pig – we found it difficult to ride away.

Eventually, when we wheeled our machines up the cobbled street, out of the village and to the top of the hill on the other side, the children followed behind, a very noisy escort. We felt like four pied pipers luring them away from their homes.

The first part of that day's ride was towards the old Roman town of Trier. We saw no isolated farm houses or cottages. The hamlets and villages looked dilapidated and poor. Many of the houses had been damaged by shells or bombs, or bore traces of bullet-scarring. The children were invariably thin. The men who sped past on motorbikes had set, grim faces.

However, when we'd passed Trier, changing some money and buying food in the market, then rode along the banks of the Moselle river, the atmosphere changed. We felt as if we were in a different country.

The surrounding hills, covered in vines, were in vivid contrast to the grey rocks and deeper greens of the forest behind. Men, wearing army khaki and black forage caps, and women, their heads covered by kerchiefs, worked with scythes and rakes in the hayfields beside the orchards and neat vegetable gardens.

Small fishing-boats, steamers and ferry-boats rode beyond the willows, reeds and pebbly beaches. Boys wearing round caps, bright-coloured shirts and short leather trousers, and girls with long white stockings beneath their dresses and aprons, hair floating behind in fair plaits, sped past. They were all friendly and waved cheerfully at us.

Now that we were on a good, flattish road, and with Esme's bike mended, it was as though we'd suddenly taken wings. We felt as free as birds as we swooped past the picturesque little grey stone towns and villages. We seemed to have cycled many joyous kilometres that day in the lovely wine-growing valley of the Moselle.

Alas, it was too good to last. When we reached the bridge at Bernkastel-Kues, a particularly attractive wine town, Barbara came to a sudden, dramatic stop. Her front tyre was flat. We decided to find a garage rather than try and mend it ourselves, especially as, in addition, Agnes's bike had started to rattle during the last few kilometres.

Our troubles were beginning again. After a meal in a restaurant, the sky turned black and within a few minutes rain was spluttering over the cobblestones. This became a flood as the force of the downpour increased.

We quickly found shelter in a wash-house which adjoined the garage where the two bikes were being mended.

Barbara tried to explain our presence there to a woman climbing the steps to the house above. When she finished, the woman unexpectedly asked if we'd like to spend the night in her house. She told Barbara it would cost five marks each.

Also – and this was the real carrot – her husband drove a milk lorry. She told us that he would take the four of us, plus our bikes, up the mountain behind at four o'clock the following morning.

It was too good a chance to miss. Before long, we were standing in a clean, well-furnished room containing two large beds and one small one.

We settled down early, after collecting the bikes. We were tired and it was too wet to explore the town anyway. The woman promised Barbara that she would call us at the same time as her husband got up.

'We must not oversleep!' Agnes put the watch on the table beside her so that its tick was close to her ear. 'We'll have to get up about three.'

12

THE RHINE

But of course we did. All the cycling and fresh air had worn us out.

Again it was Agnes who roused us, shouting, 'IT'S TEN PAST FOUR!'

I, thinking that we'd probably have to miss the lorry, snuggled further down into the warm feather bed. But by now, Agnes was standing by the window, looking down into the street.

'There's no lorry there – but there's a man. He's smoking a cigarette. WAIT!' Her voice should have awakened the town at least as she pushed open the window.

'ATTENTION! STOP! Oh, he's walking away. Barbara – do come!'

Barbara, not at all pleased at having to leave the comfortable bed, stumbled across the floor, groaning and rubbing her eyes as she tried to think out the correct sentence.

We other three waited expectantly for the words to be squeezed out, rather like toothpaste out of a nearly-finished tube.

'*Bitte ewarten Sie. Wir wenden in zehn minuten kommen.*'

Fortunately, these words seemed to work. The man in the street stopped, then replied gruffly, '*Ja, ja.*'

Esme suggested hopefully from her part of the bed that perhaps he was the wrong man and didn't know what she was talking about. But Agnes would not allow this. Who else would be about at this time? The four of us would have to dress quickly and pack our things. Washing tackle and pyjamas were thrown jumbled anyhow into our panniers and baskets and somehow squeezed down so that these could be closed.

'We'll have to wash later,' Agnes told us as she flew out of the door.

I would probably have forgotten to pay had not the landlady suddenly appeared at the wash-house door, her blue eyes round with surprise. I quickly gave her what I hoped was the right amount. As there was no Barbara there to interpret, it was too complicated to try and ask her why she had not called us and where was her husband and the milk lorry.

I found a distressed Esme a few yards down the road, picking her lipstick and hair-curlers out of the gutter. The basket on her bike, only half-fastened on, had fallen off, to burst its contents all over the road.

'The lorry's in the town square,' she pointed agitatedly, as if terrified she might be left behind.

Still wondering how they'd managed to interpret 'town square' from those two '*ja*'s we'd heard, and guided by the sound of clinking milk bottles, I ran into the cobbled centre. The lorry was standing in front of the gabled jeweller's shop. The golden hands of the clock pointed to twenty minutes past four.

I thought that Barbara must have misunderstood the woman, or that she'd forgotten to tell her husband, but I was wrong. When Agnes said, 'Mountain up,' raising an arm in a dramatic flourish, he nodded casually.

However, as he climbed up into his high seat, turning his broad back on us, it seemed that he expected us to help ourselves.

At that moment, a sturdy fellow, carrying a rucksack and wheeling a bike, appeared auspiciously out of a side-turning. He told Barbara that he'd been staying at a hostel on the hill. After he'd heaved his bike on the back, amongst the urns and crates of milk bottles, he helped us with ours.

Barbara, because of her German, sat in front with the driver. Esme, still flustered and pink with agitation, squeezed in beside her.

There was hardly any space for us on the open lorry. Agnes and the cyclist just managed to find room. I had to stand on one leg because it was not possible for me to put down two feet together. Then, by holding on to a cycle with one hand and the side of the lorry with another, I managed to achieve a degree of safety.

Oh, it was bitterly cold, and grew even colder when the lorry left the town and climbed higher and higher up the mountainside, crawling slowly between groves of firs, spruce and pine. The engine coughed and spluttered. At one point, the driver had to get out and fill a bucket of water from a stream to cool it. Even so, getting this lift had been a real stroke of luck. We had not realised how steep this mountain was and could never have climbed it with our equipment-laden machines.

But the ride had a price, which I paid. When the cyclist dismounted at the crossroads, near Morbach, I was almost frozen stiff and had to be lifted down and thumped and pummelled by the others to revive my circulation.

The young German insisted on shaking hands with us. To our dismay, we noticed that he had two fingers missing.

'Lost in plane. Boom! Boom!' He grinned cheerfully.

Then it was '*Auf Wiedersehen*', he waved and pedalled off.

Agnes gazed at the signpost and started to pull the map out her pocket when Barbara, who had been speaking to the driver, told her to put it away.

'He says he'll take us further. When he's finished delivering the milk, he's going to visit his brother who lives beside the Rhine.'

This was a real, and unexpected, bonus. It would save us much time. Also, as the crates of milk were delivered, so there was more space at the back. And as the day progressed, so it got warmer. It must have been about midday when our taciturn but useful driver finally set us down at the Rhineland resort of Bingen.

His brother's house lay to the north of the town and the beginning of the best part of the Rhine. Here was the start of the tourist route with its rugged, rocky cliffs, gorges and old wine towns. Our way was to the Rheingau, the upper Rhine, where the water widened, resembling a small sea.

There was the corresponding seaside atmosphere. The waterway seemed filled with hooting river traffic while holidaymakers crowded the banks. Blaring bands added their noisy music to the fun.

'It's a bit too much like Hampstead Heath on a bank holiday,' Esme remarked.

We eventually found a *gusthaus*, where we had breakfast in a heavily furnished and dark dining room. The walls bore odd trophies – a stuffed wild cat, an eagle, two squirrels and a pair of deer's antlers. However, breakfast tasted wonderful and we were able to have a wash in the basin on the landing.

As it was still early morning, we had to continue on our journey just to keep warm. We cycled on a while beside the Rhine and selected a place to stop where we erected our tent. It seemed perfect and for the first time the sun was shining and we were able to bask in its warmth. We decided to remain here awhile, relax and wash some of our clothes.

Barbara seemed to be the only one amongst us who could manage the erratic Primus stove. Although she did not understand its workings, she operated it by instinct rather than by scientific method. Therefore she could not explain the procedure to us. She was apt to get excited so we others kept out of the way when she was preparing a meal. We were just glad to eat it when it finally arrived.

The following day starting late as usual, we cycled to Mainz, where we visited a bank and did some shopping. Mainz, which had suffered badly from the bombing, was the first big town we reached on the Rhine. Its centre was as flat as a field; its cathedral, and churches, desolate ruins. Wild flowers and other hardy weeds had spread themselves over most of the ground. It was as if the countryside had stolen back into the town, reclaiming the land it had once lost.

We bought some oranges at a fruit stall, then continued on to Oppenheim, where we bought an ice-cream each. By now, evening had descended again and it was time to look for a campsite.

We rode on until we'd left the houses and strolling people behind. Then Agnes suggested we take a pathway between trees and reeds that led to a field beyond.

This was surprisingly hidden away: it was deserted except for a tiny house near the river. We were not sure that the field belonged to the house but it seemed as if it might. Agnes had been trained by her camper father to always ask the landowner's permission before erecting a tent on their property. The owner would also be able to supply drinking-water.

When Barbara and I knocked rather nervously at the door, it was answered by a small, rather dirty-looking, unkempt man, holding a dog on a chain.

'OK, OK,' he replied, grinning at Barbara's rather stilted request for his permission to camp in the field.

I drew some water from a tap behind the house while Agnes and Esme began to erect the tent. But as Barbara started on her task of cooking the evening meal, small insects, perhaps attracted by the Primus stove and the smell of food, buzzed round her head and tried to settle on her.

'They're probably mosquitoes or midges,' Agnes said, watching them closely. She included insects in her philanthropy towards all living things and became so upset if we other three slaughtered earwigs, ants and caterpillars that now, to spare her feelings, we removed them from clothing and bedding, and gently placed them on the ground outside. Fortunately for us, she felt no friendship towards mosquitoes.

'You can kill as many as you like,' she told Barbara indulgently, who anyway was already slashing at them with a knife.

'In fact, I'm not sure if it's wise to camp so close to a backwater,' she added thoughtfully.

Well, we were all tired, the tent had been erected and we didn't feel like moving. Esme, Barbara and I told Agnes this in no uncertain way.

'Perhaps they'll go away when we blow out the candle and close the tent door.' Agnes tried to sound optimistic.

But before we settled down for the night, I thought I saw the man from the little house, who we didn't quite trust, creeping towards our tent.

Barbara clutched the knife and called out, '*Wir sind Engländer*,' hoping that this might give us some protection.

At this, the dim shape laughed and said something Barbara could not understand.

13

HAVEN AFTER A STORM

Perhaps the little man from the house had been coming to warn us about the mosquitoes. We had a terrible night.

Agnes had shut the tent flaps to keep the mosquitoes out so that it was very stuffy inside. Even so, many of them had managed to creep in unnoticed and hide in dark corners, beneath our panniers and baskets.

A few emerged stealthily at first. Then they seemed to arrive in their hundreds. They screamed, they zoomed, they dive-bombed, like a fleet of midget aircraft. When we tried to hide ourselves away inside our sleeping-bags, they became even noisier and angrier in their frustration. They must have known that we couldn't exist without air for long, so they swarmed round each one in turn, as if they knew which nose was coming out to breathe next. We were probably the best meal of fresh meat those Rhine mosquitoes had ever dined on in their lives.

Eventually we could stand it no longer; we were defeated. Tired as we were from cycling and lack of sleep, at about three-thirty in the morning, when the grass was still asparkle with dew and only a few birds were twittering in the trees, we rose, packed our baggage and departed.

But worse was yet to come. Mosquitoes are light-footed creatures, which can land, drink, then escape, often unnoticed. Many had managed to creep into our sleeping-bags. The result of their orgy did not appear until later. It was not until a few hours had passed that we realised – and felt – the full savagery of their attack.

We were now riding towards Heidelberg, where Agnes's contact, Dr Ernst Muller, lived. When we stopped at last to eat a frugal breakfast by the wayside – it was too early for any café to be open – Agnes silently got out her hand-mirror, which we passed gloomily round.

'I've got about ten bites on my face and neck alone,' Agnes said, trying to view herself with philosophical detachment.

Barbara did not appear to have so many as Agnes, but the ones she did have were much larger. I had a particularly vicious one just above my right eyelid, which Esme laughingly told me made me look as if I were leering.

Esme adopted a rather unsympathetic attitude about our bites, probably because her face had apparently been miraculously untouched.

'I daresay it was because my bed was more hidden away than any of yours,' she told us loftily.

'You wait,' I warned her darkly. 'Yours will probably be far worse than ours when they do come up.'

Unfortunately for Esme, my prophecy proved correct. Later when the four of us rode into Mannheim, her face was redder and even more swollen than ours.

Mannheim, set between the Rhine and Neckar rivers, made up part of the dull, flattish industrial areas through which our route to Heidelberg took us. Along with Ludwigshafen, it had been so badly bombed that it was almost non-existent as a town. Nevertheless there were many people about, mostly quite well dressed but grim faced. Never before had we seen so many one-armed, one-legged men in such a small area. Although the Germans had started the war and some might said they deserved what they had inflicted on other people, only a heart of stone could not be filled with despair by the surrounding devastation. This human misery, added to the effects of the mosquito bites, put us in very low spirits indeed. But in spite of the widespread destruction, we found the people in the shops that were still open surprisingly friendly and not at all antagonistic towards us.

In fact, when I got out the secret purse to pay for some bacon in the butcher's, the man behind the counter actually waved my money aside, saying, 'It is good. The English are poor, too.'

Once upon a time, Mannheim had been a beautiful city with well-laid-out gardens and large public buildings. Now its rubble-strewn centre was crammed with noisy, badly directed traffic. The roads were confusingly marked and we caught our cycle wheels in the tramlines. We all came off at least once, Esme cutting herself quite badly. This, of course, added further to our misery.

Eventually Barbara approached an American army officer, who was accompanied by two friends, to ask the way. 'Heidelberg?' she said.

Thinking she was German, he answered her question in that language. To her delight, his accent was almost the same as hers and she was able to understand him better than anyone else she'd yet met in Germany. He, too, was pleased to meet someone who understood him with so little trouble. His friends, who only spoke English, gazed at him with admiration.

It was not until we finally rode off that Barbara remembered to turn and shout, '*Wir sind Engländer!*' to his unbelieving surprise.

This incident made us laugh and forget our troubles for a while. Our spirits were gradually reviving. More especially because Barbara had got his instructions right and we found ourselves riding out of this wretched city and on the way to Heidelberg.

In contrast, Heidelberg, Germany's oldest and most famous university town, picturesquely situated between wooded heights and the Neckar before it flows into the Rhine, was undamaged by the war.

Ernst Muller's house, a rather severe stone building surrounded by a garden filled with sweet-smelling roses, lay on its outskirts.

Barbara, Esme and I waited by the gate, letting Agnes walk down the path to the front door on her own. We could hear voices and glimpsed a woman's figure behind Agnes's tall one.

Then, 'Come on,' our leader called to us.

The four of us entered the house.

Ernst Muller was out, so it was his gentle-faced, rather frail-looking wife who met us first. She must have had very bad eyesight, not much helped by the heavy glasses she wore, because she did not seem to notice the state of our faces.

In a spell of good timing, although it was unintentional, we had arrived about lunch-time. She insisted, in spite of Barbara's protestation that we had plenty of food in our basket, that we partake of the rissoles, fried potatoes and bread already set out.

So before long we were sitting on four of the straight-backed military-type chairs. The brass studs down their centre gleamed like buttons on a soldier's coat. An enormous white Samoyard dog watched us suspiciously from a basket in one corner of the room.

Although Frau Muller explained simply that her English was not as good as her husband's, she did manage with the help of Barbara and her own dictionary to tell us quite a lot about herself.

It seemed that she had once lived in eastern Germany, where her parents had owned a large estate.

'But when the Russians came at the end of the war, it was not safe, you understand, for young women.'

She had to flee from her home and was lucky enough to fall in with a company of English soldiers. That was when she started to learn English. In return for their protection, she did their cooking and washing.

'I had no money: it was a difficult time. Then I got work in a hospital, which was very hard, but it was there that I met my husband.'

While she was talking, the large white dog climbed out of its basket to pad across the room and nuzzle her knee. She caressed him gently.

'My parents sent him on to me later. They could not keep such a large dog. He is now all that I have of my old life.'

In spite of his size, he was a clever creature and could do a variety of tricks for his mistress. When Ernst Muller finally arrived home, we were watching the dog stand and walk a little on his hind legs.

We could not have met Dr Muller, a medical man, at a more appropriate time. After Agnes's preamble and explanations as to our presence, he broke in to say, 'How nice you've come. But what is the matter with your faces?'

'Mosquito bites,' I put in quickly before Agnes had time to launch into a long description of how and why it had happened.

'How painful!' He turned out to be a man of few words but quick deeds. Before long, the four of us were standing in his small surgery, where he found some lotion to reduce the swelling and soothe the pain.

He was a sincere, good-hearted person and probably younger than his white hair suggested. He did not seem at all embittered by his experiences in a Nazi concentration camp. He had been an opponent of Naziism and so, like many others of similar views, was sent to a camp, where he was allowed to use his medical skills.

'Things are bad here,' he told us later as we drank coffee in the dining room. 'Two million are unemployed just now. But times have been worse and will get better. This zone, the American one, is the best one to live in because there was less fighting and bombing here.

'The Germans are very orderly people, perhaps too orderly for their own good. But it is still not safe for travellers, especially young girls like you on your own,' he added warningly.

This was chiefly because there were displaced persons roaming the Black Forest, our next destination and not so very far away now.

'Some of these people are unable to return to their own country; there are others who have fled from the Russian zone. They have no money or papers and cannot get employment.'

Although Agnes assured him that we had nothing worth stealing and that our equipment was too old for anyone to want, he told us that we should only camp at proper, recognised campsites.

'There is a good one at Titisee by the lake. It's a beauty spot. I'll take you there by car,' he promised. Later in the afternoon, he loaded the bikes on the roof of the car.

He explained again when he set us down at Titisee that evening that not only was it not safe for girls to camp in Germany on their own, but that it was also '*verboten*' to camp anywhere in Germany except at a proper *Zeltplatz* because of the danger to trees and crops from fire.

Nevertheless, we didn't stop long at the site after he'd driven off. We found the official *Zeltplatz* too crowded, noisy and dirty. Instead we took a path through fields massed with cotton flax, harebells and clover up the mountainside and pitched our tent beside a wide track.

14

THE BLACK FOREST

This place, where we stopped for a few days, turned out to be one of our best and happiest sites. It was a welcome rest after two very early morning rises. We were able to recover peacefully from our mosquito bites. We washed our clothes again, our hair, ourselves, and lazed in the sun; and prepared ourselves for the long journey which still lay ahead.

On our first morning there we were awakened by what sounded like fairy music. We discovered that it was the tinkling bells of animals as they were driven up the mountainside. The cows wore large bells, the goats medium-sized ones, and the two black sheep small ones. All these bells jangled together like some elfin orchestra.

It was a truly beautiful place and so quiet after the tumult of the German roads. We were surrounded by undulating green hills, their slopes hidden beneath fir, spruce and pines. Just below was a farmhouse and a grey-roofed hotel so we were not too far away from people, complying with Agnes's rule about always camping near a house. Further down still was Lake Titisee, rippling and glistening in the sunshine. The Feldberg, tipped with snow and the highest point in the Black Forest, loomed above the trees and water. Just behind us was a forest, very dark inside, and with a floor that swarmed with busy ants. These had amassed great mounds of needles, some even higher than our tent.

Our campsite was situated in a fairly public place. Guests from the hotel walked up the track to the mountain behind, a local beauty spot. They did not seem to mind our being English and they were not at all hostile. If anything, they were too friendly! One woman brought me a bowl of cherries; another one even looked inside the tent when Barbara was washing – to her great annoyance. Then they seemed to call everything they looked at '*Schön*' (beautiful). '*Schön, schön!*' was a favourite phrase. The view, Lake Titisee, Germany, even our tent, was '*Schön*'.

We had a strange visitor on the second day. I wondered if he might be a DP (displaced person), except that he didn't seem to be hiding from anyone. He came from the direction of the forest behind us. He wore very short leather shorts and a green hunting jacket, unbuttoned and untidy, and he would have been nice-looking but for the queer, strained expression in his eyes. He had only one arm, and asked Barbara if she would mind strapping his watch on for him, which she did as gently as she could.

When he sat down with us, Agnes offered him some tea, which he drank as if he didn't like it but was too polite to spit it out.

His conversation was limited as he only knew a few English words, such as 'darling', which he used a lot. Barbara began to find his attentions to her rather a nuisance but he eventually wandered off when she and Esme went to do some washing. I felt rather sorry for him. He seemed to be some sort of farm-worker, but what sort of work could he do with only one arm?

The four of us had fallen into the pattern of our allocated jobs quite well. Barbara was still cook although she did tend to get rather irritable with our tiny Primus. I, the treasurer, had also become chief washer-upper. I was also the party's recorder: that is, I tried to write up my diary every day. Agnes and Esme saw to the tent – or, rather, Agnes did most of this, but was too good-natured to complain.

Perhaps Esme didn't help as much as she should have done, but she'd had all this trouble with her bike and got very tired. Also she was the youngest and less used to looking after herself than us other three. We forgave her, realising that she probably found our roaming gypsy life a great deal tougher than she anticipated it would be.

However, it was our last afternoon at this idyllic site when disaster struck her. Esme was busy washing her hair in the brook that flowed alongside the track when we other three heard her let out a truly terrifying scream.

15

AN UNEXPECTED FEAST

Esme had lost her passport!

I at once thought of the one-armed man, now sure he must be a DP. Only I hadn't seen him go anywhere near Esme's panniers. Also, what use would a girl's passport be to him, unless he needed it for someone else, or to sell, maybe? But what sort of desperate character would rob those who had been kind enough to strap on his watch and offer him tea?

However, my suspicions were unfounded. What had really happened, Esme explained, was that her passport had fallen out of her pocket while she was washing her hair in the pool below the waterfall. This pool, a natural and convenient wash-basin, cascaded down into the swirling, gurgling stream below. Her passport was already being swiftly borne down into the great Lake Titisee itself.

Esme was panic stricken, as were we other three. We all raced down the hillside, following the course of the leaping, plunging brook. Then I suddenly spotted it, a flash of blue – Esme's precious identity – sticking lengthways out of a bank of mud and half-held by a hanging bramble.

Esme gave a delighted yell and pulled it out quickly. It was sopping wet, of course. She had to try and dry it as well as she could with one of her clean hankies. Page two, which bore her description, was almost detached and the writing on it smudged. Even her photo was scarcely recognisable.

Poor Esme was almost in tears as she relit the Primus and held the drenched book over the tiny flame for a while. Then she stuck in the loose pages with sticky tape.

'Perhaps if you always go behind us they won't bother to look at your book,' Agnes suggested comfortingly. 'Anyway, you've found it which proves you did have one, even if it is a bit wet and torn,' she added.

Esme nodded. But she decided to leave the washed out pages alone in case she was accused of tampering.

'I'll just have to explain what happened each time we come to a frontier.' As the next one would be Austria, she hoped that Barbara would be able to work out the right words by then.

Still, in spite of this unfortunate incident, neither Esme nor we worried for long. We all felt rested: our clothes were clean again; our mosquito bites had subsided and stopped itching.

When we finally set off from this site, many people from the hotel below had gathered to watch us take down the tent. They gave us a rousing cheer and shouted '*Auf Wiedersehen*' to encourage us on our way. Even the one-armed man, who I had so unjustly suspected, emerged briefly from the forest behind, to wave his one arm, then blow a kiss, quite delicately, in Barbara's direction.

Our spirits continued to rise as we cycled through the Black Forest. The rounded mountains, mantled in firs and spruce on every side, looked so neat and well cared for that we might have been riding through one vast wooded park – the Schwarzwald, as the Black Forest was called. It was all so '*schön, schön*'. I even found myself wondering if mischievous goblins and dwarves dwelt in the shadows of the tall trees.

We felt so happy we started to sing. The sun was shining. We must have completed over 1,000 miles of our long journey. Next would come Austria, Italy (oh, romantic Italy!), France, Spain and then France again.

By now, we had discarded our thick divided skirts and windjammers. Instead we wore brightly flowered seersucker skirts and nylon blouses.

Then Agnes and Esme, cycling two abreast, got in the way of a car. The motorist hooted angrily as he sped by. But even his red and scowling face could not dampen our high spirits.

Later, when we stopped at the crossroads to look at our map again, we found the angry driver's car drawn up as if awaiting our arrival. But the angry driver had changed into a fat, jolly holiday-maker beneath a wide white floppy hat and wearing a blue-checked open-necked shirt. His companion, who we'd not noticed before, was also dressed in casual holiday attire. He had a pale but not unpleasant face. They asked if they could help.

Neither of the men could speak much English but they did have an excellent map. We were coming to the end of our current one. Radolfzell, our next destination, was just off it. I was planning to buy another when we found the right shop.

It didn't take much persuasion for us to follow the two men into a nearby café and look at their map, which they spread out over a table.

They were most intrigued about our journey. Barbara found herself trying to answer many questions, such as 'Where are you going next?' and 'Where do you intend to stay the night?'

She explained slowly in German that we were going to Austria and that we had a tent.

'*Ein Zelt*!' said Heini, the fat, jolly one, who we discovered was a butcher from Frankfurt. His companion Rudolph – he owned a garage somewhere – frowned. It would be too cold a night for a *Zelt*. Besides it might rain. Also camping in Germany wasn't safe now, especially for women. This was becoming a familiar warning. We should sleep in a *gusthaus*. He knew of a good one.

Barbara told him quite firmly that this was out of the question. The tent was our temporary home: we were used to it now. Also *gusthaus*es cost money. We were trying to travel economically.

When the two men realised at last that they couldn't change our minds, they invited us to supper. Also, Heini beamed, he knew of a good site he'd take us to.

So much for a good site. After a short drive with us following behind their car, it turned out to be quite unsuitable for camping. It was too isolated – there was no house nearby for protection, or from which to obtain drinking-water. And the land there was too sloping to pitch a tent on.

Heini and Rudolph climbed back into the car disappointed. Then Rudolph had an idea. It seemed he knew of a *Zeltplatz* not far from Lake Konstanz.

This new place they led us to was not perfect. Although uncrowded and with a house near at hand, it lay between the main road and the water's edge. The savage mosquito attack we'd undergone beside the Rhine was still fresh in our memory. Even so, we decided it would have to do.

Heini and Rudolph sat on the grass, watching with amusement as Agnes and Esme put up the tent. They found it hard to believe that anyone could actually like sleeping in a tent.

The two girls, perhaps determined to convert them to camping, erected our tent with the greatest of care. It looked as beautiful as a tent could look when they'd finished – neat, symmetrical, without a wrinkle in the material, and not a guy line too loose or too taut.

'Now for a meal,' Heini told Barbara, still grinning.

To our great surprise, he opened the car door and after the two men had shuffled inside for a few minutes, they emerged with their arms full of sausages, long loaves of bread and bottles of beer. They deposited all this food and drink inside the tent, where we all gathered.

We were utterly amazed. Food had been rationed in Britain for years. And never before had we seen so many different kinds of sausages. There were long ones, short ones, fat ones, thin ones, black ones, brown ones. Heini was not a butcher for nothing.

'*Sehr gut?*' he chuckled, watching our faces.

'*Sehr gut!*' we murmured hungrily.

However, although Heini and Rudolph tried their best it soon became obvious that neither of them were, nor ever would be, 'camping types'. Heini, in his corner next to Barbara, looked overweight and out of place, although he did his best to smile and appear happy. Perspiration trickled down his plump face. Rudolph, next to Esme, did not even try to pretend he was comfortable. He fanned himself with his handkerchief and gazed longingly at the door, which I had closed to keep out what mosquitoes there were about.

It was difficult to do justice to the food and try and converse, using gestures and the aid of one small dictionary. Barbara did her best to keep up a dignified conversation with Heini, who seemed very taken with her. He insisted on stroking her back ardently with one hand while he looked up the appropriate romantic words in the dictionary with the other. I could see my sister beginning to lose her temper. Especially as, being the only German-speaking one amongst us, the whole burden of conversation fell on her.

Rudolph, who had spread himself out on my green Lilo and was flirting with Esme, was trying to behave like some eastern sultan with his slave girl.

Agnes and I counted ourselves lucky. As the two gooseberries or 'maiden aunts', we were able to enjoy the food without having to put up with any of the bother.

Fortunately for us all, perhaps, the tent was really too small for two large men and four girls, even when we were only sitting. Heini gradually became more and more disillusioned with camping, and possibly with Barbara, too. He had to fan himself continuously with his large handkerchief.

Rudolph's legs were too long anyway for a reclining sultan in such a limited space. Suddenly, red-faced and cramped, he got up and stumbled over to the door, which he undid – letting in a flurry of mosquitoes. We heard him stamping about and belching outside.

Finally, the two men decided to go. They had had enough of camping and '*Zelte*'. It was too uncomfortable, crowded and hot. They pretended to be sorry to have to leave. Heini even pointed to the tent as he stumbled out, saying, '*Ein gutes Zelt.*'

'Well, they've left the food.' Agnes was triumphant as she surveyed our groundsheet. It was still littered with the considerable remains of the sausages, bread and beer.

'It'll last us for days,' I exclaimed jubilantly.

PART THREE

16

FIRST CAMPSITE IN AUSTRIA

We took the steamer across Lake Konstanz to Austria the following day, leaving the first boat at Lindau, where we had to go through customs.

As anticipated, Esme had difficulty in explaining her damaged passport to the puzzled officials . Even when Barbara came to her assistance they were hard-pressed to understand. In the end she and Esme tried to mime the incident. The frontier officials appeared quite fascinated by their gyrations. Stooping, stretching and waving their arms, they might have been performing some weird, exotic Eastern dance as they tried to recreate the effect of a rushing stream bearing away Esme's passport, .

Still, some good did come of it because as a small crowd gathered round us to watch, a tall dark Austrian, who spoke some English, was encouraged to come to our aid. He was later able to give us some useful information about Austria and, in particular, Bregenz, which was our next destination.

In spite of the strong wind blowing, it was a most enjoyable trip across the lake and a welcome rest from cycling. It was my chance to send a card to our brother Gordon and also write up some more of my diary. I found it quite a task to remember all that we'd done and I needed to write it up fairly quickly before I forgot and a nearer event pushed out my memory of the one before.

Esme wrote a postcard to her parents. She had some difficulty in knowing what to put. 'I'd better not mention the lift in the lorry nor the mosquitoes as that would probably worry my mother,' she told me, then added, chuckling, 'And if I ever told them about Rudolph and Heini and the sausages, her ears would probably fall off.'

She wrote at first: 'My new bike is terrible,' then crossed this out as she thought it might upset her father, who'd chosen and bought it.

Finally, she simply put: 'Dear parents, having a wonderful time. Will write again when we get to Florence. Lots of love, Esme.'

While Esme and I were busy talking and writing, Barbara was experiencing some problems with our new friend, the Austrian man. She had discovered that Austro-German was sufficiently different to German to undo much of the progress she'd made while travelling through Germany.

However, with Agnes's help and a diagram, she managed to pin down the whereabouts of a good hostel in Bregenz. If we stayed there overnight, we'd be able to make a really early start the following day for the next leg of our journey – Austria and the Tyrolean Alps.

According to our guidebook, the Tyrol, completely hedged in by mountains, straddles the frontier between Austria and Italy. It is a region of snow-capped peaks and rugged heights, fertile valleys, flowery pastures, rushing torrents, tiny streams, and quaint towns and villages. In fact, the guidebook enthused, it is one of the most magnificently picturesque areas of Europe.

Bregenz, once an important Roman trading post called Brigantes, lies beside Lake Konstanz in the wooded foothills before the Tyrol's western edge.

We left the hostel early the following morning as planned. But first I had to visit a bank to change a traveller's cheque and also the German marks into Austrian schillings. We had decided to make towards Innsbruck, capital of the Austrian Tyrol, and which would probably take a few days to reach.

By now, it was swelteringly hot. Not only were we considerably further south but it was also well into summer.

Barbara, Esme and myself had put on shorts and Agnes a lighter skirt, which we found more comfortable for cycling. But putting on lighter clothes brought new problems. Where could we pack the heavier clothes we'd taken off? Space in our panniers and baskets was so limited that it was almost impossible to put in anything larger than that which had been taken out. This meant that overflow clothes and heavy walking shoes (replaced by sandals) had to be tied onto our carriers and handlebars, giving our expedition a somewhat clumsy, old-clothes-for-sale appearance.

This was especially so of Agnes's bike. On top of her panniers, square black basket, small clothes basket and long strap handbag went her folded tweed skirt and walking shoes. In addition to all this, she carried our Primus stove paraffin, which swirled around in its bottle like an angry mauve sea. How she managed to move at all, how her old bike didn't collapse under the strain, was a mystery to her three friends.

However, cycling is a very peaceful way of travelling: the countryside only changes gradually. One is a more leisurely part of it than when in a car. There is more time to think and look around.

Once beyond Bregenz, we started to compare this new terrain with the Germany we'd just left behind. There were quite a few external differences. The fields, for instance, appeared less rigidly cultivated. There was a more congenial atmosphere of untidiness and gaiety. People had darker skin and hair, smiled more often, seemed more vivacious.

Many of the houses, usually built mostly of wood, were decorated with hanging baskets of flowers and bright flower-filled window boxes. Some of the stone houses had an entire wall painted with a scene from the life of a saint. There were also numerous roadside shrines to remind us that Austria was a predominantly Roman Catholic country.

Our first campsite was in a sloping field and once again in front of a stretch of forest. This time, though, there was a schoolhouse below instead of a hotel. The caretaker let us use its tap for drinking-water.

Oh, and how we dined in style that evening! Not only did we have the remains of Heini and Rudolph's sausages, but we ate to the soothing, melodious strains of Viennese waltzes wafting up from a radio further down the hill.

17

THE AUSTRIAN TYROL

We had planned to make an early morning start so that we could put in as many miles as possible before the heat of the midday sun made cycling too tiring.

Yet we still found striking camp early difficult to do unless propelled by some external circumstance like escaping from mosquitoes.

Firstly, that following day, we dawdled around the tent after moving it further backwards into the long shadow cast by the forest. A cooler Esme then wrote another postcard, this time to friends in her old office – probably telling them a lot more than she had told her parents.

Then we all went shopping together. The shops here seemed fairly well stocked but quite expensive. Trying to deal with the continuous changes in currency was beginning to make me feel quite giddy. Usually I, the treasurer, and Barbara, the cook, shopped together. Barbara would try and plan out a meal while I worked out the cost. Barbara would start off in German but quite soon as the right words and phrases escaped her, she would merely point wearily to the desired commodity. Sometimes we argued so heatedly about what we should buy that Agnes and Esme, if present, would make some sort of conversation with the shopkeeper, hoping to divert his or her attention away from our bad behaviour.

Agnes liked to follow me round with a notebook in which she put down everything we spent. This should have been my job but sometimes I forgot, especially when it was hot, and later made up the figures. Agnes, so honest herself, never suspected this. When her figures didn't balance she would grumble about how bad she was at maths.

We finally left this site about one o'clock and rode towards Bludenz. By now, the sun was scorching. We had decided that it would be quite impossible for us to climb the mountain ahead with our heavy bikes; also the roads were bad. Instead we caught a train to St Anton. From there to Innsbruck, we would be cycling downhill all the way.

The train ride proved a wonderful journey and by far the best way to travel through mountain scenery. We sat outside on the platform at the back of the train, where it was fresh and cool as the train slowly wound its way up into the snow-capped heights.

St Anton, a well-known ski resort perched about 1,290 metres above sea level, is situated at the start of the Tyrol. So we felt that it was fitting that we should begin the Austrian leg of our journey from there.

Although it was great to be riding downhill instead of laboriously climbing up, the road was too rough and chippy for us to let go of our brakes and whiz.

Then there was the accident.

Agnes, whose faith in traffic often seemed as strong as it was in people, had the bad habit of sometimes zigzagging when she rode. She was frequently on the lookout for something useful, such as an old piece of string (she had once picked up an abandoned piece of pyjama cord) to replace a broken strap, or to tie something extra onto one of the bikes. Or maybe a piece of wire to wind round a broken cycle spoke. Or a nail. Or some small thing that she thought we might need. It was partly the result of the war and her make-do-and-mend upbringing, and partly the challenge it presented to her ingenuity. This didn't matter too much if it were Barbara or I behind her. Unfortunately Esme was short-sighted but disliked wearing her glasses when cycling.

On this occasion, Agnes suddenly drew up sharply to allow a column of ants to cross the road. Esme crashed into her. As Barbara and I were too close to avoid them or brake quickly enough, we crashed, too. The four of us folded up together like a concertina, a real motorway pile-up! Fortunately, the road was empty of traffic. There were no broken bones, only bruises.

Although we continued on again after we'd got ourselves together, we were badly shaken.

The road still sloped downwards, thankfully. Also, the grey clouds swirling round the distant peaks, threatening a downpour, only developed into a light drizzle, which did not last long.

The scenery through which we were now passing was truly magnificent and continually changing its contours. Sometimes we would be riding beside sloping verdurous fields, where the newly-gathered hay, twisted round poles, resembled little men. Then we would be enclosed by slate-grey mountains, where only the sturdiest of trees could push their way between the boulders. We cycled for many miles alongside a river, greeny-grey and topped with foam, racing against us over the stones.

When we finally drew up that evening in a small town, the weather had become uncertain again.

'I don't think we should risk camping tonight,' Agnes said, gazing up, worried by the grey-black puffs of clouds, drifting round the tallest peaks. Heavy storms can erupt suddenly in mountain areas: streams swollen by torrential rain can bring swift disaster to campers, sweeping away their tent and equipment, and maybe, sometimes, themselves.

'Where can we stay?' Barbara wondered aloud, looking round at the old houses. Lights gleamed through windows onto the cobbled street. Sounds of music and dancing flooded out through one open doorway.

While we were debating what was the best thing to do, a motorcyclist suddenly clattered up to us. Its rider was a rough-looking fellow, shabbily dressed, but with a jolly vivacious face. He gallantly asked if he could be of any service.

'A *gusthaus*?' Agnes said simply.

'Ah.' He rubbed his hands together, apparently delighted that he could be of some help. He told us that he knew of a place that was 'gut und billig' and led us to a nearby inn, where an iron lamb swung high above the doorway. Alas, as it was quite late, it was already full up.

However, we were not to despair. After some discussion with the girl at the door, who he seemed to know, he beckoned us to follow him down the street to a house at the end.

The door was answered by a thin, white-haired woman, already clad in her dressing-gown. After gestures and gesticulations, she indicated that we unload our machines and put them in a shed at the side of the building.

This done, we followed her into a sloping-roofed passage. She put one finger to her mouth and pointed to our shoes. We were to creep. As silently as Red Indians, we crept through the hall into a bedroom, which to our surprise was already occupied by two males.

'Only young boys,' the motorcyclist told Barbara when we reached the room beyond. This was clean and well furnished – a washstand, two white bolstered beds, a divan, polished wood furniture and flower pots containing drooping ferns beneath the window.

And – the motorcyclist pulled a key out of the door and waved it triumphantly aloft – we could lock ourselves in if we wished.

Next for a meal. As usual we were starving. The motorcyclist led us off down the street, back to the Gasthof Lamm, where he dashingly kissed Agnes's hand beneath the swinging emblem. He told us regretfully that he had to return to Innsbruck but would stop with us for three minutes.

The Gasthof Lamm could be described as a typically Austrian inn. The tables and surrounding benches were separated from each other by tall walls, making intimate compartments, lit by a dim lamp, which a black-haired merman clasped lovingly to his stomach. Deer antler trophies hung from the ceiling; a crucifix, decorated with stale browning corn-cobs, was suspended above a pot of ferns.

Once seated, we learned that the motorcyclist was called Franz and that he worked as a swimming instructor at Innsbruck.

After he'd ordered a meal and red wine for us, he suddenly placed his watch on the table – a reminder that he only had three minutes.

But these three minutes proved to be very long ones. His watch ticked on unnoticed.

'We must go,' Agnes stood up at last. She was worried about the woman in the dressing-gown, who would have to let us in and might have gone to bed. We would also have to creep past the two boys again, without waking them up.

'*Nein!*' Franz made a theatrical gesture of despair, then motioned for us to wait. He left us briefly to return with two young men – his friends, he said. They would sing and play to us. One of them had a guitar tucked under one arm.

Franz seated himself beside Agnes while Barbara found the guitarist on her left. His friend, quite a handsome fellow with long eyelashes, in spite of a scar beneath one eye, sat next to Esme.

The guitarist began to play in a melancholy fashion, while the other man sang to a blushing but flattered Esme.

Franz, who wore two rings on his fingers – for he had two *Lieblings*, he had told us earlier, one in Munich and one in Salzburg – removed them with a flourish. He assured Agnes that he was now quite free.

But we four were too exhausted by our cycling to feel romantic about anyone. And the red wine had made us sleepy.

Also, we knew so little of each other's languages, there was no way we could communicate.

Agnes repeated that we'd have to go, but this time more emphatically and with us others backing her up.

So, after many grand protests and toastings, we were finally escorted by the three men back to the house at the end of the street.

The woman let us in quietly. We tiptoed past the two boys, now gently snoring. Soft guitar music floated through the window just when we were about to climb into our beds. But this died down when we switched off the light.

'Well, that's the end of that,' Agnes spoke thankfully from the divan.

Or so she thought.

18

INNSBRUCK

About two hours later, I was awakened by Agnes's startled voice.

'There's a man in the room!'

It was the singer from the Gasthof Lamm.

When first I, then Esme, sat up in our shared bed, we saw his figure sitting on our piled up luggage. He was smoking a cigarette and speaking softly in Austro-German. We heard the name 'Esme' mentioned.

'He's yours!' Both Agnes and I turned on the poor girl accusingly.

But even if he were, we would still have to get rid of him. How could this be done? All our protests were ignored, wilfully misunderstood. Only Barbara spoke enough German to tell him to go away properly in his own language. And she was still fast asleep.

Agnes ran over to the other bed and shook her vigorously. Alas, tending to be a heavy sleeper anyway and now partly doped by the wine, Barbara was really out. It was only after I had pummelled her and Agnes had shouted 'THERE'S A MAN IN THE ROOM!' as loudly as she could down her earhole that she opened her eyes.

'Well, why did you let him in?' she asked indignantly when his presence in the room finally registered.

We didn't bother to argue the injustice of this insinuation. Instead we begged her to tell him to go away. She sat up slowly while we waited for what seemed an interminable time as she searched her mind for the appropriate sentence. Then out came, '*Verslassen Sie unser Schlafzimmer*,' which was simple enough and obvious too, for she pointed to the window. Then, 'Get out!' in English as indignation overcame her.

But he ignored Barbara's order. He did not even move his position. Instead he started, rather contemptuously, to blow neat cigarette rings in our direction.

'What shall we do? We can't leave him here all night,' Agnes wailed in despair.

It was our Esme who decided to take some positive action. She must have felt some responsibility for his presence as it was her name he was calling. Suddenly and unexpectedly she jumped out of bed and stood beside the agitated Agnes.

'Get out!' she spoke firmly, as if she were addressing a naughty child.

He sniggered and lunged towards her, making her step sideways to avoid him. In doing so, she found herself standing beside the washstand. It was then that she noticed the heavy china jug.

'GET OUT!' she repeated more firmly. Picking up the jug, she advanced with it towards him.

He remained where he was, watching her playfully.

Then carefully and to our startled but admiring horror, she emptied the contents of the jug over him. The water went splashing through his hair and down his suit on to our panniers and baskets.

He was so surprised that he didn't move until the jug was emptied, when he leapt to his feet, shook himself, and swore at her.

'*RAUS! RAUS!*' Barbara, recalling more German, shouted from the bed.

Then Agnes remembered the two boys asleep in the room next door.

'Tell him about those two boys,' she urged Barbara.

'*Kinder.*' Barbara's mind, perhaps still blurred, was working along different lines to Agnes's. 'You'll awaken the children,' she told him in German.

'Not *Kinder*!' Agnes almost exploded. 'They're men! See!' She unlocked the door and flung it open. 'There's a man in our room,' she informed the two inmates dramatically.

Two very embarrassed young boys, not much more than twelve or thirteen, rolled out of bed and padded barefoot to the doorway. Fortunately, they were learning English at school. After Agnes had explained the situation, they exchanged a few words with the angry, dripping man.

'He is drunk,' one of them told us seriously. 'He says he will go away when he has finished his cigarette.' Rather miraculously, this was still alight.

So, after the two boys had returned once more behind the key, the four of us sat silently on the beds waiting for him to finish and to go. Agnes also thoughtfully opened the window wider and removed some of the pots of ferns to make his exit easier.

He finally crushed the cigarette end out on the floor. Then with a spring he was outside. A pile of wood clattered below. He was gone.

Agnes shut the window and locked it.

We all four woke the following morning with splitting headaches – a result of the wine we'd consumed, sleeping with the window shut, and last night's excitement.

We never saw Franz and his two friends again. Also, by the time we'd washed, dressed and packed, the two boys in the room next door had left. I paid the woman, who was still wearing a dressing-gown.

Our ride to Innsbruck was quite enjoyable with only a few hills to negotiate. Innsbruck, the mountaineer's city, seemed to spread itself out all around the valley as we descended towards it. At first, the surrounding mountains were hidden in clouds. When these drifted slowly upwards, they rose like a flimsy curtain to reveal the sheer shimmering grey and white wall of the mighty northern Alps.

Tired and hot, Barbara, Esme and I stepped into the first bank we saw in the town to change another traveller's cheque, leaving Agnes to guard the bikes. When we emerged from its cool stony interior, it was to find an excited and perspiring friend.

'Guess who I've met?' She beamed in delight, without expecting an answer, as it was unlikely that any of us other three would have known them.

It transpired that two camping acquaintances from England had just walked by. Frank, a tall, dark, bespectacled, rather studious-looking fellow, and Tom, also tall, but very fair – both in their early twenties – stepped forward to be introduced.

The two men were camping at a site on the outskirts of Innsbruck and were able to guide us there.

Quite a few English people were staying at this site. In one way, this was a welcome relief, like arriving home; but in another, it was a let-down. It miffed us to see so many tents just like our own. The neat rows of sturdy, well-pitched tents exuded an air of calm, sweet order. To match their regularity, Agnes and Esme set up ours with extra care. After all, Agnes had her family's camping reputation to keep up.

Still, staying there a while made a pleasant rest and gave us another chance to prepare ourselves for the adventures that still lay ahead. 'Tent Town', as we called it, was very peaceful. There was no chance here of a pig, a swarm of mosquitoes, or any other unwanted visitors in our tent. It was safe and rather dull.

We enjoyed exploring Innsbruck, a particularly picturesque city with many old cobbled streets, archways, courtyards and cheerful window boxes. We strolled down the famous Maria-Theresien-Strasse and the busy, narrow Herzog-Friedrich-Strasse, gazing into the shop windows. We learned from the studious Frank that the Goldenes Dach (little golden roof) was added to the building which took the place of the ducal palace in 1500. Legend says that it was erected by a penniless Tyrolean duke who had had it covered with golden coins because he was pretending to be rich. In reality, it dates from the reign of the Hapsburg Maximilian I, and symbolises the power of the Hapsburgs, who used it as a royal lodge from which to watch performances given by players on the square below.

We also took the opportunity to visit the Poste Restante where letters can be sent when people are travelling abroad. Most cities and large towns have this department in their main Post Office. Barbara and I found a brief note from Gordon, which did not tell us much. Esme also received a long and instructive letter from her mother. Agnes, most disappointingly, found nothing at all.

Later that day, Esme and I took eight pairs of shoes to the cobbler near the site to be mended. This was a reminder of all the times we'd had to walk, pushing our bikes.

On one day, Frank and Tom took the four of us on an excursion up into Innsbruck's surrounding mountains. We rode above the city in a wobbly funicular, getting a new view of its rows of houses, green domes, red roofs and the river Inn, snaking through like a curling grey road.

These two boys turned out to be real friends. Not only did they take us to places they themselves had already visited, but they also insisted they examine and, if necessary, mend our bikes before we continued on our long journey.

It was discovered, as a result of their inspection, that: my handlebars were out of alignment, turned to the right and that I had somehow adapted myself to this lopsidedness; Barbara's carrier had slipped so far down from the weight of her panniers that it was pinning down her back brake; and it was a wonder that Esme could ride at all with her speed-gear jammed so high. As for Agnes's bike, it was a case on its own.

'A bit old,' Frank commented at last. He didn't want to hurt her feelings. 'I suppose it might just last you out the tour.'

Agnes, who must have identified with it in some way, tossed her head and looked quite indignant for her machine.

'It's been in our family for years,' she said firmly, as if this was a guarantee that it would last forever.

PART FOUR

SWITZERLAND

AUSTRIA

DOLOMITES
*Bolzano
*Trento

ITALY

*Verona *Venice

Genoa

Ravenna

*Rimini

Marseilles

Florence
Pisa*

LIGURIAN SEA

19

A BROKEN TENT POLE

'*Dov'è la vostra casa?*' asked the official at the Italian frontier; where were we staying?

As yet it was too soon after the war for many foreigners to take their holidays in Italy. Four young females on their own, and intending to camp, was something quite extraordinary to Italian frontier guards.

We had left the camp early that morning after having faced a battery of cameras. Frank had taken a movie of our departure, which was to be included in his film about his camping holiday at Innsbruck. Tom had taken a number of snapshots, especially of Barbara. When we'd finally ridden away from the large audience of campers who had collected to see us off, we felt as if we were departing royalty, or films stars at least.

We'd taken the train from Innsbruck up the mountains to the Brenner Pass. It had proved a beautiful journey, first passing through valleys, then climbing slowly beside the tall peaks to the Brenner Zee, a low cool lake set in their shadows. Again we had sat outside on the platform where the air was refreshing. When we had arrived at our station, the guard had helped us down with our baggage and bikes, then blown us a kiss – a last Austrian gesture – before the train had continued on its way.

Although the Austrian officials looked shabby in their green uniforms, they were quick and efficient. But as small children were playing on the barrier, using it as a sort of seesaw, we had to squeeze our machines through a narrow gangway. Then a short walk down the road and we were in Italy.

Almost immediately, two officials in smart uniforms and braided hats, as handsome as film stars, came forward to snatch our bikes and cycle passbooks out of our hands, shouting '*Presto! Presto!*' We carried these passbooks with our passports. Nobody had bothered much about them before.

To our dismay, our passports were whisked away, too, and we were directed to another hut, where men seemed to be working with noisy vigour.

And this was where the man behind the grille in front of his counter rapped out his question to Esme.

'*Dov'è la vostra casa?*' It was Esme this time because we had pushed her, very unwillingly, forward. After all, her mother was supposed to be half-Italian. Although Esme had not been able to visit Italy yet, because of the war, we felt she might know something of the language, even if it were only the pronunciation.

'*Dov'è la vostra casa?*' the man repeated impatiently. Then '*Presto! Presto!*'

But by now, Esme felt too hot and tired to be cooperative. She shrugged wearily as if she had not the faintest idea what he was talking about. The crowd now collecting behind was growing restive. Fortunately for us, and everyone else, a friendly American colonel, standing nearby, translated the sentence for her.

'He says where are you staying.'

'We have a tent,' Esme explained diffidently.

'A tent!' The colonel raised bushy eyebrows.

'*Hanno una tenda.*'

The busy work in the hut suddenly came to a stop as if someone had blown a whistle. The men downed what they were doing to listen. The man behind the grille rattled off another sentence like a machine-gun firing.

'He says where are you going with your tent.' The American colonel was beginning to look embarrassed as another spate of words erupted from the official. 'Because he says he and a few others are coming off duty soon...'

However, perhaps for the best, the official did not wait for an answer. As if suddenly remembering his position of authority, he started to shout, '*Passaporto! Passaporto!*' as if he were trying to subdue a restless crowd.

We left the hut limply, exhausted but determined to try and get back our passports from the hut into which they had disappeared. There would probably follow the difficulty of explaining about Esme's damaged one.

Happily this was unexpectedly resolved without Esme having to go through the antics of her exotic Eastern dance again. The two officials at the barrier had seen us coming and pushed their way roughly through an indignant crowd. To our surprise they picked up our passports from a desk then recovered the cycle passbooks from elsewhere in the hut. Then it was '*Presto! Presto!*' again, as they returned all this plus the bikes with many bold flourishes.

'Phew! So this is Italy!' Agnes wiped her forehead and glared at Esme as if having a half-Italian mother made her personally responsible for the apparently irrational behaviour of the inhabitants.

She became angrier still when, as we cycled off, a passing car splashed her with water as it sped through a puddle. Instead of apologising, the occupants of the car only laughed and waved gaily. It was just their idea of good fun.

Still, Agnes was too good-natured to be annoyed for long. And we were all very taken with the majestic grandeur of the surrounding Dolomite scenery.

The mountains, a curious blend of earth pyramids and ancient glaciers, had been fashioned through the ages by erosion and weathered into a variety of extraordinary rock formations, such as ragged or needle-shaped peaks, archways and even towers and domes. A mixture of pinkish lime and magnesium in the stone made them shimmer and shine in the sunlight, adding even more to their beauty.

However, although it was wonderful to cycle through this magnificent range – the river flowing alongside, often through caverns cut in the rocks – it was not good camping country. The sides of the mountains were too steep and the few pieces of flat land too cultivated. We had to ride miles between their rugged splendour before we could see any place that might be suitable.

Agnes finally drew up before a farmhouse perched on a round hill. There was the possibility that there might be some land behind it, which we could use.

This time it was Esme who was made to climb the steep path to the door. I ran after her to help because I'd learned Latin at school, and words I'd seen on Italian posters looked similar to Latin, even if they would probably be spoken differently.

Neither of us had much confidence in the sentence provided in our international phrase book – 'Kindly permit me to erect my tent in your field' – which sounded more like a military command then a polite request.

Esme knocked. There was a long interval before the door was opened, very slowly, and only halfway at that. A sturdy, heavily-built woman peered suspiciously out at us.

Esme bravely read the sentence aloud in her best pronunciation, but there was no change of expression, no spark of understanding in the woman's face. She stared craftily first at Esme and then at me and shook her head.

In desperation, Esme handed her the book and pointed to the sentence. The woman held the book away from herself then turned it round so that it was upside-down and flicked vaguely through the pages.

'Perhaps she thinks we're trying to sell her something,' I suggested, trying to be helpful.

'It's very obvious she can't read,' Esme retorted, exasperated.

The woman suddenly handed the book back to her, saying 'Nein, nein, nein.'

'*Nein* – German!' I called urgently down the hill to Barbara.

However, the woman having spoken once, was not to be tempted again, especially by Barbara's German. She was not exactly hostile, only dull and uncomprehending.

'*Tenda, Zelt*, tent.' By now, Agnes had joined us, too, using what languages she knew. She even tried to describe the shape of a tent with her arms.

'*Compris*?' At last, despairing.

The woman nodded. She understood 'Compris' if nothing else.

Agnes didn't give up easily. She picked up a stick and began to draw a tent in the dust. It was no use. The woman did not follow. We decided to move on.

But at least we had aroused her interest. She left the safety of her doorway and walked to the top of her garden. She stared after us, still mystified, a solid apathetic figure among the rows of cabbages and other vegetables.

We found a campsite in the end. It was Agnes's sharp eyes that espied it.

'Look!' She drew up suddenly and pointed to some land where the hay had been cut and a few thin goats were nibbling at the stubbly grass. Unfortunately, it lay on the other side of the river and although there was a bridge across it, it was difficult to see how we could reach the bridge across the fields from the road we were on.

'How can we get down there?' Agnes pondered.

While we were puzzling this out, we saw the goats being rounded up by a whistling boy who guided them on a clear and deliberate route through the fields.

'There must be a path,' Agnes said excitedly.

There was, although we took some time to find it.

After we had cycled over the bridge and found another path, we arrived in a very poor village. Ragged, barefoot children were playing in the street. Women were standing in the doorways of their houses, or around the carved stone fountain. A few men were lounging idly about. They stared at us curiously as we pushed our way through, an unlikely convoy.

Beyond the village, the road tailed off into a narrow lane beside a railway track. We followed this until we came to a tunnel. After we had persevered through its darkness, we emerged at last into this flat field we'd seen on the other side of the river.

In some ways it was a perfect site. A row of alders and young poplars grew beside the river, forming a slight screen from the roadway, whose telegraph poles we could see running along the side of the mountain opposite. Although our field could be seen quite easily from the road, we knew it would be difficult for anyone to find their way down to it.

A white wall, which we thought was a house, gleamed thorough the trees to our right. Agnes and Esme set off to find its owner, while Barbara and I started to unpack the bikes.

But our luck had run out. The house turned out to be the remains of a burned-out barn. Even so, Agnes decided to waive her rule about always camping near a house. After all, there was a village not too far away, even though it seemed to be a very rundown, dilapidated and poor sort of place.

Later, when Barbara and I set out to fill our water bag at the stone fountain, we were stopped halfway by a boy on a bike. He pointed anxiously to the clouds that hung over the mountain peaks, then tried to indicate by signs and gestures that we should sleep in the village.

We thought that perhaps he imagined we intended to sleep in the open. I tried to reassure him with the aid of the phrase book that we would be all right, even if it rained, as we had a tent.

'Tenda. Si. Si.' He shrugged doubtfully, then rode off.

The village appeared quite deserted when we arrived in its long street again. It was uncannily quiet compared to the noisiness of only about an hour ago. We both felt nervous, as if many eyes were watching us from behind the crumbling stone walls of the houses. We filled the waterbag quickly and returned to the site.

Back here Agnes and Esme were having difficulty in pitching the tent on a ground which was considerably harder than it looked. There was an electric tension in the air which made us feel irritable and apprehensive. The clouds that had gathered overhead were now drifting down the side of the mountains, combing through the trees, slowly enshrouding them in mist. It was becoming windy, too.

Darkness descended early that night. Later when the tent was finally set up and we were eating our meal of macaroni and cheese in what we believed was its safety, Agnes had to light a candle, the stand of which we affixed to a pole. Its cheery flicker somewhat offset the gloom outside.

'That's better. At least we can see what we're eating.' I tried to sound cheerful.

Then it happened. Suddenly a green sheet of lightning lit up the sky. Next a flash of thunder, like a bomb bursting, exploded overhead. Almost immediately we were engulfed in a raging storm. Fierce gusts of wind shook the tent as if it were a mere toy while pounding rain seemed to be trying to force its way through the thin material.

Oh, but much worse was to follow. As we sat in frightened silence, hoping and praying that this storm would soon pass over, we heard a low whistling sound like a small tornado rushing though the grass. Our tent was whipped off the ground. Fortunately, its pegs held and the tent was dropped before the mini tornado continued on its wild way.

But the strain had been too much for one of our slender bamboo poles. This cracked, then split in two, and our tent home collapsed on top of us.

20

NIGHT IN A PRISON CELL

I kept my head throughout the chaos. As I was nearest the candle attached to a pole, I managed to prevent it falling against the tent's flimsy material. Then, feeling rather like Atlas balancing the world on his shoulders, I somehow held up the falling tent on my back.

Barbara, Agnes and Esme were literally rolling about at my feet, spilling their plates of macaroni and cheese all over the bedding. We had been saved temporarily but what should we do? We were in a real dilemma. With one of the tent poles broken, one side of the tent was unsupported unless I remained where I was all night. And where on earth could we find another pole in the Italian Dolomites at night in the middle of a storm?

It was Esme who unexpectedly came to the rescue. She suggested we make a splint. She said she'd seen a few pieces of wood lying around outside. Then, without even waiting for an answer, she crawled past me as I was already starting to complain. She returned a few minutes later, dripping wet and carrying some sticks.

Gradually we all recovered from the shock. Agnes, in particular, had been almost paralysed with horror. She selected the most suitable stick from those Esme had gathered, then bound a piece of string she'd picked up somewhere in the road round it and the broken tent pole.

'I hope that's safe.' She gingerly released it to let it prop up the sagging half of the tent on its own. With great relief, I was able to unbend from my uncomfortable position.

The other three crossed their fingers and hoped that this very frail and makeshift arrangement would hold. The storm was beginning to die down now: its worst was over. We scooped the macaroni and pieces of cheese off our bedding and onto our plates – we couldn't afford to be too fussy – finished our interrupted meal and settled down to sleep.

When we awoke the following morning, the sky was innocently blue – not a cloud to be seen – and the sun was shining, just as if nothing had happened. The only evidence of the storm's fury was the dampness of the tent and the surrounding springy turf and, of course, our temporarily-mended pole.

We decided to make an early start before the goats returned to reclaim their territory. Furthermore we didn't want to spend more time than was necessary in these treacherous mountains, especially with our rickety, skew-whiff tent.

Treacherous or not, it was impossible not to be impressed by the continuing grandeur of the surrounding scenery. There was a wildness about these peaks, so unscalable and coldly aloof, that was quite different from the Tyrol we'd seen and certainly unlike the neat, almost park-like appearance of the Black Forest of our earlier journey.

But the scenery changed gradually as we progressed through it. At first, we were riding through high mountain gorges, where brooks trickled lazily or dashed in a frenzy onto barren ridges; and with an occasional castle standing in solitude, square and with pointed towers, a warning to invading armies. Then we descended slowly onto a wide plain, passing fields of tobacco, maize and corn, or heaps of hay, with lines of grapevines clinging to the undulating hills beyond. The river lay to one side, bold, swift and grey.

By now, the chief colours of the countryside were changing. Grey rocks were being replaced by reddish-brown earth. There were more vines and stretches of sunflowers. The red-tiled roofs of the houses glowed warmly against their white walls.

Effigies of saints, often quite ugly and garishly painted, added their impassive presence to the vividness of the scene.

Although we had enjoyed the rugged beauty of the lonely peaks, we were pleased to be amongst people again. But it was noisy. And this got worse, especially when hot afternoon turned into cooler evening. The traffic on the road, so swift and aggressive, increased in numbers. Cars and lorries swerved dangerously past, blaring their horns.

We were soon obliged to give up watching the passing scenery. Except perhaps Barbara, our romantic, who liked to paint, and was especially taken with the Italian landscape.

We seemed to fly along. This time I was leading. It had irked me that Agnes should always take the lead, although this was bound to be so as she had the strongest legs. But although thin, I was wiry and quite strong with little body weight to carry, so I did sometimes manage to cycle ahead. Esme had her own rather unhurried, laid-back style, but always got there in the end. Barbara, a dawdler, liked to daydream. But today we were all keeping as close to the side of the road as we could. Any slight wobble to the left would have resulted in an immediate collision with an overtaking vehicle.

As treasurer, I did let my thoughts wander a bit. We had not yet managed to pass a bank that was open and I had little money left in the secret purse. We'd bought a loaf of bread at the last village but one, using up some of the lire I'd managed to change with Tom back at the camp in Innsbruck. It looked as if this, plus some butter and some tea without milk, would have to be enough for our evening meal. That is, unless we opened our emergency tin of sardines. I supposed if we didn't pass an open bank this would constitute an emergency. While I was pondering on this my thoughts were suddenly interrupted by a real emergency. Agnes was anxiously shouting at me from behind to stop.

'Now what?' was my first thought. I wondered whose machine could possibly have broken down this time, especially after all the attention they'd received from Frank and Tom.

I turned to see Agnes and Esme talking excitedly to a gesticulating man on a motorbike a few yards down the road.

'It's Barbara. There's been an accident.' Agnes's face was quite white beneath her sunburn. 'We've got to go back.'

We three returned hastily, scared, not knowing what we would find.

Barbara had been riding dreamily at the back of the line when the road suddenly narrowed. On one side of her was traffic, on the other a steep precipice. There was sand along the precipice edge and she knew, like the rest of us, that if her bike wheels touched this, they would go into a skid.

Suddenly two cars and a lorry had chased down the road. There was room for the three of them, but not for her, too. She told us she had to choose between a collision and the sand. She closed her eyes. She felt a crunch, sailed over her handlebars and down the mountainside.

Her fall was checked by two forked bushes, so she ended up on her back, as helpless as an upside-down beetle. All that could be seen of her from the road must have been the soles of her feet sticking through the leaves.

The two cars continued on, but the lorry stopped. Two men climbed out. They could see her machine and baggage lying in the roadway. Only Barbara, the rider, had disappeared.

'*Signorina, signorina, dov'è, dov'è?*' they shouted and one of them climbed down towards her. Then he and the other man formed a human chain to pull her up – by one leg only – back into the roadway.

Agnes, Esme and I were very relieved when we eventually came across Barbara sitting on one of the white teeth placed at intervals along the road. She looked pale and was picking brambles out of her legs and arms. Her bike, lying beside her, was miraculously undamaged.

'I wasn't really hurt, just shaken,' she told us after recounting her adventure. 'And I'd been expecting this to happen for so long that it was quite a relief to get it over with.'

After she had fully recovered and her two rescuers had driven off, the four of us continued on our way again, but riding even more carefully than before. We wouldn't quickly forget that if it hadn't been for two small forked bushes sticking out of the mountainside, we might well have lost one member of our party.

As it grew darker the traffic slackened, but heavy clouds formed above and it began to rain.

'We'll have to camp,' I told them. Barbara's accident had temporarily put our financial position out of my mind. Now there was the worry of our wobbly tent pole. And, as the rain spattered down increasingly heavily, it looked very much as if we would have to camp in a puddle.

Agnes sighed. She was beginning to feel that our disasters were more than she could cope with. 'If we go on a bit we might find a dry spot.' Her voice sounded more optimistic than I guessed she felt.

Needless to say, we didn't; neither did the rain show any signs of easing off. If anything, it became heavier. There was also the added danger of being struck by lightning if we camped near a tree in a thunderstorm.

It was well and truly evening, almost nightfall, when Agnes and I, a little ahead of the other two, cycled through the streets of what looked like the beginning of a small town.

We both stopped – as though by telepathy – outside a pair of wide iron gates. By now, a strong wind was blowing, billowing out our white capes like the sails of a ship. Perhaps the wind had blown us there. A friendly light flickered through the house's hallway, out onto the cobblestoned courtyard beyond.

'We could ask the people inside to help. They might have a barn we could use,' Agnes suggested.

Esme and Barbara, now almost blown towards us and dripping wet, agreed.

So, leaving Esme – who now firmly declared that she knew no Italian at all – to guard the bikes, we other three entered the building and walked down a stone passage. Doors either side made it resemble a narrow street.

Agnes chose one door and knocked. This was opened to reveal a very tall man who stared at us, not too surprisingly, in amazement. And no, he did not speak English, nor German, nor French, nor anything but Italian. His wife and two tall red-haired sons, who presently joined him, also shook their heads.

But wait. There was hope! The man put his finger to his mouth and bid us follow him quietly through the kitchen and living room into a small darkened room beyond. We glimpsed a bed in the corner where an elderly woman lay, covered by a blanket.

The man motioned us not to go too near. So we three knelt at the foot of the bed, our white capes dripping pools on the stone floor. It seemed the woman could understand written English, but she could not speak. He pointed to her throat. She was ill.

Agnes wrote quickly in her neat handwriting that we were four girls without any money, that we had a tent but with one broken tent pole, that the ground outside was covered in puddles. Had they a barn in which we could sleep? The note was handed to the woman. She read it slowly, nodding, then in a trembling, spidery hand, she wrote her translation for the man to read.

In a flash, all was understood. Within minutes, we were bundled through the kitchen and living room out into the hallway. The two tall sons whisked the cycles out of Esme's dripping protection and pushed them into a wash house amongst mangles and tubs.

Then the man flung open a door not far from his own. Two red-quilted beds stood in a bare, whitewashed room. A small barred window looked down at us from the opposite end.

'Non è bello, ma...' He shrugged, smiling. It was nothing special but the best he could offer us on this stormy night.

It must have been a very favourable wind indeed that blew us there because the storm increased in ferocity, making the electric lights turn off, then on, then off again.

Signor T, as we called him, struggling to pronounce his surname, was kindness itself, as were his wife and two sons. After Signor T had found an English/Italian dictionary, we were able to communicate more easily. We learned that the sick woman was his mother. He wouldn't let us see her again in case we excited her and made her talk. She understood English because she had taught it in school. Signor T also gave us a better sentence than the one in our phrase book for asking people if we could camp on their land, which would come in very handy the next time we were looking for somewhere to pitch our tent.

The following day he took us on a tour of the building, which, when seen by daylight, was much larger than we had realised. He was the caretaker. It was the local court house. Our bedroom, so fortunately unoccupied that night, was the cell in which people who'd been arrested and were awaiting trial were kept overnight.

Two resident guests at the building were a pair of swallows which nested above the lampshade in the passage. Neither Signor T, nor his wife, seemed at all worried by the mess they made on the floor. In fact, they were pleased that the birds returned to their summer house every year as they were supposed to bring good luck.

We hoped that the good luck would spread to us on the next leg of our journey. We certainly needed it.

21

TOWARDS VENICE

Venice was our next goal and we were all looking forward to our first visit to this so-called Queen of Cities. It was founded many centuries ago, so the guidebook I'd bought at Trento noted, by people fleeing from invaders on the mainland. They settled on the marshes and the lagoons, which they had to enlarge and strengthen with piles of wood and stones. Their city eventually became an independent republic, later ruled by a dux or doge. After many fierce struggles, it became one of the wealthiest and most powerful states in Europe. Times change. Today's Venice probably makes most of its money from tourism.

As we now felt quite rich after cashing another of our traveller's cheques at Trento and the surrounding land was too built-over for camping – not forgetting the problem posed by our rickety tent pole – we decided to spend our next night in a pensione. As usual, though, we left it too late to be choosy: descending darkness forced us to stop and spend the night at a particularly smelly and ramshackle village.

Agnes, ever optimistic, asked some men we saw lounging about outside a shabby *pensione* if it were '*bella*'. '*Bella*', like '*schön*' in German, seemed to be a word that covered anything not too bad in Italy. They replied '*Molto bella! Molto bella!*', but rather as if they were referring to her than to the inn she was pointing at.

Its chain door jangled to let through a dark girl, her hair set in a stiff, fuzzy style. When she saw us and the bikes, she threw up her hands and screamed. But after we'd explained that we wanted to spend the night in her *pensione*, she became quite friendly and indicated we store our bikes in the cellar below. This accomplished, she clapped her hands and shooed away the men who were now pressing round us.

She eventually turned out to be such an agreeable person that Agnes could not resist trying to tell her about our journey in as descriptive and dramatic fashion as she could in her limited Italian. This made the girl scream in horror at us once again. Then we heard her rush outside and shout to the listening crowd. '*Belgio, Lussemburgo, Germania, Austria, Italia – quattro signore con biciclette!*'

We had a good meal of spaghetti and fruit, although when Barbara ordered some fruit which was out of season, this made the girl scream even more at us. As the door behind her kept opening and shutting for people to peer in and gaze, she had to continually put down what she was doing and drive them away.

The *pensione* was large and spread out with landings as wide as rooms, filled with chairs and tables and flowerpots. When we had breakfast the following morning in yet another room of this sprawling inn, the bill was much larger than I had expected. Perhaps in recompense, the girl presented us with a postcard of Lake Garda.

It was a beautiful day with not a suspicion of rain when we crossed Lake Garda. The water and the sky were the same brilliant blues as on our postcard. Our boat dropped anchor lazily at the little towns and villages set around the water's edge. It was such a peaceful change from cycling, just to watch the passing scenery, talk, laze and rest without the constant fear of being knocked down by a speeding car.

That night's campsite was beside the small port of Desenzano, near a café. There was no rain, no thunder and not much wind. Our mended tent pole held up well, though the tent's shape had lost that perfect symmetry of which Agnes and Esme had been so proud. This, alas, was something it never recovered.

Our next day's journey was to the old Roman town of Verona, about forty kilometres away. From there, we planned to take the train to Venice.

Unfortunately the train ride to Venice proved to be a much slower journey than we'd anticipated and we did not arrive until evening. Once there, although there were plenty of porters around, none of them would give us a hand with our baggage and bikes. Eventually Barbara and I took matters into our own hands and commandeered a trolley we saw standing idly by.

None of the men bothered to stop us. The porters, recognisable by their long black overalls, merely left off talking to watch what we would do next.

'No *biciclette* in *Venezia*,' a few shouted as we wheeled our reloaded machines over to the exit.

There followed a noisy fracas. We were feeling too hot and tired to think properly. When a man grabbed my bike as some kind of joke, I thought he was trying to steal it and shouted angrily to the other three to come to my aid. Next Barbara lost her temper when a porter almost dropped a pile of parcels on top of her. Furious, she started to hurl them back at him. Poor Agnes, although very hot and flustered herself, tried to calm Barbara and the porter down.

'Perhaps Esme and I had better try and find a hostel,' she said at last, wiping her perspiring forehead. Fortunately, by then she had managed to persuade Barbara to sit down on a bench and the porter to go away.

Probably because of the war, when people couldn't travel, we were very ignorant. Our knowledge of European geography must have been very slight. We were learning about places as we went along. We knew that Venice was a lovely, dreamy old city, honeycombed with waterways and bridges, but had not realised that what the amused porters were trying to tell us was that you couldn't use bicycles, or any sort of vehicles there, because there were no proper roads, only lanes, squares and waterways.

When this was eventually understood, we had to unload our bikes, which we left in the station baggage office. Then Agnes and Esme, after obtaining the address of a hostel from the information office, set off into the labyrinthine city, leaving Barbara and me with the luggage (so difficult to carry without the bikes). Our tempers cooled, we sat almost listlessly on the wide station steps, surrounded by panniers, baskets, pigeons and people.

Agnes and Esme had difficulty finding a place for us to spend the night. The hostel near the Academia, a gallery containing a collection of famous paintings, was full up, with people queuing for beds. The 'Father' there rang up a similar hostel in one of the poorest parts of Venice and they made another journey in a ferry boat, but the places had gone by the time they arrived.

Fortunately, the Father of this new hostel knew of another residence, and two Italian students staying at the hostel returned with them to the station, kindly offering to help with our baggage.

Agnes and Esme had left us two there about eight o'clock: they did not return until ten-thirty. It was now too dark to appreciate this most fascinating of cities. Lights from the hotels and houses splashed shimmering bands of colour across the dark water. But there were still the unique smells and noise of Venice.

The Father from the final hostel met us at the quayside and guided us down a lane so narrow that we had to walk in single file. The hostel's entrance, lying behind a rusting iron gate and tiny courtyard, was heavily barred. The Father had to pull at an ancient jangling bell and was then carefully scrutinised through a grille – its tiny holes made it resemble a tea-strainer – before the door was opened by a woman dressed in an old-fashioned black gown, bonnet and shawl.

After she had silently beckoned us inside what must have been a female stronghold (only the Father was allowed in; the male students who'd helped us with our luggage were brusquely shooed away) she was joined by another woman, very similar to look at, except that her skin was sallower and she had a purplish mole on one side of her face.

These two sisters of the church, who walked in a curious gliding fashion, led us down the passage into a long dormitory, lit by one small electric light bulb.

This room, so cool, silent and dim, seemed uncannily quiet. After we'd undressed and were in bed, one of these ladies returned to turn out the light, her voluminous black gown flapping round her. Then she disappeared, rather magically, through a disguised door, painted the same drab colour as the wall. She put me in mind of a witch, or some sombre legendary bird. This vision persisted until I drifted into a deep sleep.

22

VENICE

Before we were able to start on our explorations, we were pushed and prodded by the two intimidating ladies of the previous night into a cell-like room near the dormitory. We had arrived too late for them to take down our details and they needed some information about us. Agnes was given a pencil and paper and the two of them indicated that they wanted our names, our addresses, our ages and our work status.

Although Agnes did her best to comply with their demands, her efforts did not seem to please them. They groaned, they sighed, they shook their heads and they wrung their hands as if she were a naughty child. Eventually, they managed to make her understand that they wanted her to write everything in block letters. So she did.

They were at once all smiles and pleased nods. They patted her on the back as if she had just managed to learn a difficult lesson.

'*Bene! Bene! Brava! Brava!*' they chanted.

In spite of their unnerving, sweeping presence and the fact that the hostel was probably situated in one of the poorest and dirtiest parts of Venice, we decided to stay here a few days.

'It's very cheap,' I told the other three. 'We only need to come back here late in the evening.'

We could spend whole days roaming the city, exploring the waterways and alleys, and visiting the palaces and piazzas, the churches and art galleries.

The next thing we had to do after filling in the forms about ourselves, was to visit a bank, which was situated in a most palatial building on the next waterfront. Our feet sank into deep pile carpets. The interior was decorated with gilded pillars and had the most intricately patterned ceilings and walls. Only the somewhat sulphurous and seaweedy smells drifting in from the canals outside marred its luxurious atmosphere.

Then, our secret purse well stuffed with lire, we took the river tram down the Grand Canal, which winds its way through the city like the letter 'S', cutting it in half. Its curving causeway was lined with old houses, lovely churches and sumptuous palaces – the elegant façade of the old Venetian nobility.

We disembarked at the Rialto bridge. Esme, who had already walked over and broken two pairs of sunglasses while camping, bought another even more decorative pair.

One day, we took the river tram to the Piazza San Marco in the centre of Venice.

The wealth of Venice was founded chiefly on piracy. The Venetian fleet travelled far abroad bringing back booty, which, along with the fabulous riches acquired by the traders, was used to decorate their beloved city. St Mark's body was stolen from Alexandria and a chapel was built to hold this sacred plunder, alongside the doges' palace. This chapel was later replaced by the enormous St Mark's church.

St Mark's, with its mosque-like domes, pillars, mosaics and luxurious carvings, looked more like an eastern temple than a church. Above, on top of the clock tower and in memory of the Christian victory over the Moslems, bronze Moors heralded each hour with their hammers – a task they had done for 500 years.

We visited the doges' palace first, a fairy-tale building in soft pink, and wandered up the Scala dei Giganti (Giants' Staircase), named not for its size but for the colossal statues of Mars and Neptune which dominated it. We next ascended the Scala d'Oro (Golden Staircase), which at one time could only be mounted by those whose names were in the Golden Book. These privileged persons were the rich merchants who, by keeping a register of all the families in their aristocratic caste, managed to maintain their hold over the doges and the people.

There was so much to see: paintings by artists such as Bellini and Tintoretto and many others whose names we forgot, and ceilings wrought in gold and brilliant colours, showing scenes from legend, the scriptures and the history of Venice. There was the great hall, the gigantic Sala del Maggior Consiglio and the enormous 'Paradiso', painted by Tintoretto and his son Domenica, reputed to be the largest picture in the world.

Agnes and I were particularly fascinated by the gruesome dark cellars below, whose barred windows looked out into the smelly canal. The Bridge of Sighs, over which so many wretched condemned prisoners must have passed, connected the palace with the state prison on the opposite side of the Rio di Palazzo.

When we eventually wandered into the piazza again, it was midday and too hot for walking. We collapsed exhausted for a while on the seats, within the cool shade of the arches.

In spite of the overpowering heat, Agnes, who could never sit still for long, was soon in conversation with one of the many men who were lounging around. This one was a particularly unsavoury and crafty-looking individual, I thought. Yet his theatrical gestures and expressive, humorous mouth gave his villainy a sort of attractiveness. He offered, very gallantly, to show us around Venice for nothing.

We had been intending to visit St Mark's interior next when we felt it was cool enough, but Agnes's new friend shook his head vehemently when we told him this. He insisted that Agnes would not be allowed inside.

Nevertheless, as I reminded them, a visit to the church was part of today's plan. So, in spite of his warnings, the four of us strolled over to the splendid edifice, sometimes unkindly described as an outsize Byzantine wedding cake.

We didn't get far. A man, a guardian of the church's morals, we supposed, stood outside to turn away any female who he considered to be improperly dressed. This seemed to mean anyone who had much bare arm showing. As many of the would-be sightseers, especially the French ones, refused to accept what they felt was a personal and arbitrary decision, quite a fuss was going on around him.

However, when he was too busy dealing with angry protesting women, Barbara, Esme and I did manage to slip past. Agnes was less lucky. Perhaps it was because she was too honest – or maybe it was more difficult for her to hide her long tanned arms behind her back. Anyway, she was denied entrance.

We others decided she had not missed much. We found the interior garish somewhat. St Mark's Basilico was the holy shrine of the Venetian state. Merchants travelling abroad were supposed to bring back a new embellishment for St Mark's and the loot from Constantinople and their enemy Genoa made it seem more Eastern than Western. The effect was dazzling and not what we thought a church should look like inside. Also, the most interesting of the mosaics, which were supposed to tell the story of the world's creation, were in the dome and difficult to see.

We liked the horses' gallery, though. From there, we could look down on the piazza below. These noble creatures represented yet more looting for they had been stolen from Rome by Constantine, later stolen from his city, Constantinople, by one of the doges, and later still stolen from Venice by Napoleon. They were returned to St Mark's in 1815 after his defeat. Unfortunately, since then, many sightseers had desecrated their golden sides by carving their initials and signatures there.

When we eventually left the church, it was to find a really furious door guard. Poor Barbara, whose sleeves were only a bit shorter than Esme's and mine, would have been detained if he'd noticed her before. As it was too late for him to do anything about it, he had to content himself with shouting abuse after us.

It was too hot for anyone to shout back. So we drifted off, trying to ignore his rudeness, and back to Agnes, who was chatting happily to our self-appointed guide.

'He says he can get us a ride in a gondola boat,' she said enthusiastically, turning to us. 'For nothing!' she added for my benefit. We found this rather amazing, especially as we had heard that the gondoliers were on strike for the day.

'I fix – you see!' Our new friend the rogue winked, then, grinning rather fiendishly through his tobacco-stained teeth, slipped off into one of the passages behind the waterfront. We realised that he was probably a scamp and a scoundrel, but it was difficult to dislike him. Anyway, it sounded like an adventure. And to visit Venice without riding in a gondola was almost unthinkable.

We waited: Agnes delighted by her success; us other three more cautious. But we were all agog to know what would happen next.

He returned not very long afterwards with two men. One was a big fellow with crisp, black, curly hair, and quite smart in neatly pressed grey trousers and spotless white shirt; the other was smaller and smooth-haired and smiled a lot, showing off his flashing white teeth. He wore white shorts and a shirt with a zipper-front. They both wore suede shoes.

They scrutinised us up and down, thoughtfully, as if we were on sale in a shop. They considered for a while, then nodded. Yes, we would apparently do.

So we left our guide, who waved us gallantly off, and – with Agnes leading, beaming – we followed, curious but cautious, down the narrow streets just off the piazza. More men, perhaps also gondoliers, gathered round us. They too looked us up and down, but shook their heads.

'No good. Trip off,' one of them remarked scornfully to me. Then, unexpectedly, our two gondoliers slipped away down a side turning and vanished from view.

We felt disappointed and cheated, and retreated hastily into a darkened chemist shop; partly to hide from these humiliating stares and partly to let Barbara buy some face powder. She had been planning to buy some anyway, and perhaps now thought it might boost her morale. It seemed that the four of us weren't considered worthy to ride in a gondola boat while a strike was on.

However, we were wrong. When we emerged into the brilliant sunshine, we met the two gondoliers again, looking flushed and angry, as if they'd been involved in an argument.

'Are you not coming with us?' the small one asked. 'It's quite safe. We will do you no harm.'

So we followed the two men down even narrower and dirtier streets to a lane of water. A long black gondola rose and fell on the slight swell.

The small gondolier unfastened it from the post and we clambered in. Agnes sat at one end with Barbara and me, while Esme sat in the centre. The big man took an oar while his friend held the pole. We glided off, slipping down lanes, past old stone houses, whose front doors opened straight out onto the water. Barred windows gave them a grim, prison-like aspect. But these were only to keep out the thieves, the big gondolier told us.

Scum floated by and the air was foul with the smell of drains, rotting vegetables and fruit, but our noses were gradually becoming used to this.

Then we suddenly came out into the Grand Canal where the water was quite rough and waves broke over the end of our slim craft. The waterway was less crowded than usual owing to the gondoliers' strike. On the opposite side were what seemed to be hundreds of their empty crafts – long, black and as slippery as whales, bobbing about like corks on the water.

'There is a strike because the authorities wish to put motors in the gondolas,' the little gondolier, who spoke quite good English, told us. We all looked suitably flabbergasted at this sacrilege.

By now, we had left the Grand Canal and were drifting through narrow waterways into a larger canal, then it was round and out towards the cooler, cleaner Adriatic sea. At first, it had seemed that our boat was the only one out here, but as our craft swung round an island, a rowing boat appeared. Our gondolier lifted his pole and hailed the two occupants.

There followed a brief conversation in Italian between the two men. Then our two gondoliers asked if two of us would mind climbing into the rowing boat as this would lighten the gondola. Agnes and I, who were weighing down our end, decided we would go. As the two boats swayed together, we stepped gingerly aboard the other craft.

Guilio and Antonio, the men in the rowing boat, both dressed in bathing trunks, had come out here to swim where the water was cleaner. They both spoke French well – they had been educated in France – and were now working as waiters in a hotel in Venice.

Antonio told Agnes and me this in French while Guilio rowed.

Suddenly, without warning, Guilio slipped the oars into their resting place and dived over the side into the water, rocking the boat. Antonio laughed, moored the craft to a pole stuck in the mud, and dived in too.

'Swim?' His dark head appeared in front of us, as sleek and shiny as a seal. He splashed and pointed to some spare trunks beneath our seat, which he suggested we use.

When we refused, Antonio returned to the boat and sat himself between us so that he could put a damp hand round each of our waists. Guilio soon followed him back into the boat. After scuffling through the bathing trunks he recovered a bag of peaches and half a loaf. We had had no lunch that day so the food was welcome. We sat and ate happily together.

But what of Barbara and Esme? When I suddenly remembered their existence, I turned to look and discovered that they were miles away. Their boat was a mere blob on the horizon.

But was that an agitated figure at one end, waving to us and signalling? Then we heard what might have been two blasts on a whistle. One of us, usually Barbara for some reason, always wore the whistle round her neck. It was really a precaution in case of accidents when cycling, or in case we lost each other in a crowd. Were those two unmistakable blasts an SOS for help? Agnes wasn't sure. I thought they might be.

'Take us over,' I ordered Antonio, nearest the oars. Agnes, now anxious, backed me up, but more placatingly so as not to hurt his feelings.

Guilio grinned and Antonio picked up the oars. He obeyed unwillingly and rowed us over, slowly, very slowly, towards the other craft.

There was certainly trouble aboard where a smouldering battle was taking place. The small gondolier had suddenly become very amorous and attacked Barbara, who, upset by its unexpectedness, had warded him off with angry blows. Both were red-faced.

I, indignant at seeing my sister abused, shouted at the little gondolier, who shouted back at me.

It was our friend Antonio who came to the rescue, speaking calmly at the small gondolier. He in turn became at first contemptuous, then sulky. Antonio suggested that he and the small gondolier change places, which they did. Peace was restored and the two crafts moved apart.

Nevertheless, a dark cloud had settled on us.

'I gentleman, I do not take your sister. She too young for me. I like proper grown woman,' the small gondolier suddenly burst out at me scornfully.

By now, we had reached a wide island, but when the gondolier suggested we land for a while, Agnes and I refused, feeling that we would probably be safer in the rocking boat.

'Let's go back to Venice,' Agnes suggested tentatively. 'We dine at six-thirty,' she added, making our probably frugal meal sound quite grand.

'No hotel dine until seven-thirty,' the small gondolier responded haughtily.

So we continued to glide across the water with the small gondolier now rowing. Venice seemed miles away, almost lost in the distant mist. The sky was stained pink by the sinking sun, while red and gold clouds tumbled together.

When Agnes asked the small gondolier to take us back to Venice again, he refused to reply. It seemed that his dignity, his manhood, had been badly bruised.

'Find a nice Italian girl,' Agnes suggested to soothe him.

'Italian girl no good,' he scoffed. 'She always ask what you earn, what your work is. English and American girls better.'

'English girls are cold,' Agnes said.

Whereupon the little gondolier grabbed her arm and pinched it. 'All women the same beef!'

Our two boats continued to drift about the sea indefinitely, interminably, it seemed. None of the rowers or gondoliers were in any particular hurry to return to the shore. Church bells were now ringing across Venice. It would soon be nine o'clock. It seemed as if we'd been on the water for hours, even days.

Finally, the two boats came together again.

'You must all get into the same boat,' Antonio ordered. But no sooner had Agnes and I clambered aboard the gondola than he and the big gondolier leapt into the rowing boat, leaving us four floundering on our own.

'Now row yourselves home,' they shouted at us gleefully.

Fortunately for us, the two gondoliers had no intention of losing their valuable craft, so they soon jumped in. Antonio and

Guilio blew kisses, waved and slid off, back towards the sea.

We circled slowly back to the Grand Canal, drifting in and out of waterways. Italians apparently had mercurial temperaments. Their moods could change so swiftly that they seldom remained angry for long. The small gondolier had completely recovered his good humour by the time we were gliding down the Grand Canal, and was singing sweetly to both Barbara and me, perched on the prow of the crowded boat.

When we eventually reached the quayside again and we four climbed out, we were all the best of friends. The expedition finally over, the gondoliers shook our hands then left, waving and singing.

23

THE LOST BIKES

The next day Esme declared most definitely that she would no longer even continue to read sentences aloud from our international phrase book. The fact that her mother was half-Italian was neither here nor there. It was her first visit to Italy, as it was ours, and she knew no more of the language than we did.

'It's too hot!' she complained. 'It's someone else's turn.'

'It won't be me,' I said firmly. 'Looking after our money and seeing that we're not short-changed needs all my attention.'

Then, out of the blue, Agnes, usually so good-natured, told us tersely we'd have to appoint a new leader. Yesterday's episode had shaken her confidence. She felt she could no longer trust her judgement.

'From now on, someone else must make the decisions – and take the blame!' she said.

That seemed to leave Barbara, who'd not yet spoken.

To our surprise, she agreed to take over Agnes's role, but we other three would have to take our share of the responsibility.

'We'll make Ravenna our next destination,' she decided, looking at our map spread over the table in the café, where we were having our breakfast. 'It's old, picturesque and has some famous mosaics. Dante once lived there. We can cycle from there to the Adriatic coast, where we'll camp.'

Camping on the coast was part, I think, of Barbara's private dream. She envisaged our finding a beautiful place beneath palm trees, a warm sea nearby in which we could swim and acres of golden sand. It was a dream she never lost sight of and probably helped to spur on her tired legs.

We other three did not really object to this vision. We were just less optimistic about finding it, that was all. Up to now, Italy had seemed to be a very noisy, overcrowded country, except for the short time we'd spent in the Dolomites, of course.

But as Ravenna was some distance away and it was extremely hot, we decided to use the railway again.

To take a train in Italy, especially with bikes, was still a fairly tricky thing to do. We had to fill in forms again. Barbara did her best to make it clear to the clerk concerned that it was absolutely essential that our bikes arrived at the same time as us, since we were obliged to change trains at Ferrara.

We did not arrive until past six o'clock in the evening. I immediately worried about our bikes, our precious steeds, without which we were stranded. I had not seen them at Ferrara although a porter there had told me they were OK. I left the luggage with the other three and quickly ran over to the baggage office.

However, the clerk there stared at me in surprise, then at the train, still in the station, when I asked him where the bikes were.

'*Biciclette*? *Niente biciclette*,' he replied as if he thought it strange I should even possess a bicycle, let alone expect to see it at Ravenna.

'What does he mean, *niente biciclette*?' Barbara, who seemed to be developing something suspiciously like an Italian temperament, asked angrily, striding over to his desk.

Again, alas, it looked as if a scene were going to take place. Interested porters and clerks put down what they were doing and gathered round to watch.

However, the luggage clerk was a patient and polite man. He explained there had been no bikes on the train. He was sorry our plans had gone astray. It was a pity. It was fate.

But we would not be so easily humoured. Agnes, in voluble French, and Barbara, in halting if precise German, struggled to express their opinions of Italian railways. The clerk nodded, agreeing. He himself knew how inefficient everything was, most especially the porters. But what could he do about it?

'Oh, it's hopeless.' Agnes was almost in tears. Our rage turned to despair. We sat dejectedly in a circle on our baggage, hoping pathetically that we were in everyone's way.

As always happens in Italy, a crowd of curious people soon collected round us, some sympathetic, some merely amused. One Italian gentleman, who spoke a little English, interrupted our indignant conversation to suggest politely that he phone the railway in Venice.

Agnes handed him the precious form. He studied it carefully. 'You have three bikes?'

'Four!' I exclaimed.

'But there are only three mentioned on this form. I am sorry.'

'Only three!' So much for Barbara's leadership. Agnes snatched the form from him to discover that the clerk in Venice had only written down three cycles. Now, not only had we no bikes here, but we could only prove that we'd ever possessed three.

'It looks as if all, or certainly one of us, will have to finish this tour by train,' I said resignedly.

The crowd had become really sympathetic. Even the porters had stopped laughing and stood around looking concerned, as if they would like to help if they could.

'At least we still have the tent!' Agnes said, surveying the baggage on which we were sitting. Everything was not entirely lost: we still had a tent in which to sleep.

After this remark, the Italian gentleman turned to a soldier standing near him and asked if he knew of a suitable site in the town where we could camp.

He did – or thought he did. For it was situated on a piece of land between four busy roads and could not have been more public than if it had been the town square itself.

Still, it was just as well that we went along to view it. While Agnes was trying to tell the soldier in her best French that it was not suitable for four *signore* and he, poor man, was struggling confusedly to listen with his other ear to Barbara, speaking in her slow German, a passing cyclist saw us and stopped.

He was a small, wiry man with spiky, close-cropped hair sticking up above a determined, elfin face.

'Can I help?' he asked, stepping nimbly off his machine. With that one sentence, he seemed to take charge of the situation.

'I am a globe-trotter from Lapland,' he told us after Agnes had explained our predicament.

This rather extraordinary statement did not particularly surprise us. After all, were we not in Italy where anything might happen?

Our rescuer bristled with such a fierce competence that everyone at the crowded station to which we'd returned seemed to obey him.

'Cycle form,' he called out to Esme, who happened to be holding it. Bemused, she handed it to him, then we all followed him into the ticket office.

Before long he was on the phone to Venice. Had they four cycles, four *signore*'s cycles? Everyone was straining to hear the answer. The station staff and as many passengers as possible crowded into the small room with as much excitement as if they were listening to the result of an important football match.

'*Si, si.*' Then they had to be sent off at once to Ravenna; '*Presto! Presto!*' There must be no delay.

After he had given this order and put down the receiver, the little Laplander had some more good news for us. It so happened – almost miraculously, it seemed to us – that he had recently opened a youth hostel in Ravenna.

'This town has always needed one. Many foreign students come here to study the mosaics,' he explained. And who better suited to be its Father than he, who could speak five languages?

So this was where we would spend our next night.

First, though, we had to load all the baskets, panniers, boxes and tent poles, which we had only just been able to carry on our four machines, onto his bike. Then, looking like he were some sort of street vendor, or a man trying to sell his home, he started to wheel it down the street. Only the top of his head showed above.

But even he, the superman, saw that it was not the practical way to move so much luggage. As suddenly as he had decided to carry it like this, he decided not to. Within a few minutes all our equipment was spread out over the pavement.

'Wait!' he ordered and left us, only to return shortly, driving a lorry.

And his efficiency didn't end there.

Later, when we'd arrived at his hostel and were sitting in his office, the walls of which were plastered with lists, directions and posters, Barbara confessed that we had no food.

The Laplander at once clapped his hands and the French student who appeared was ordered to take Barbara round the town on the back of his motorbike. It did not matter if the shops were closed.

'Go round and knock at the back,' he instructed.

We later discovered that the Laplander was not only Father of the hostel, he was also its chief chef. When the French student and Barbara reappeared with the food, he – with our help – prepared a grandiose meal.

We ate it in his office, which led off the kitchen and was also a dining room and common room combined. It was in a basement and its only ventilation was a grille window set up high in the wall. We could see people's legs passing us; sometimes inquisitive faces bent down to peer at us. The

Laplander explained that as his hostel was new in Ravenna, the inhabitants were still curious about it.

However, he did not intend to be its Father for long. He was a restless fellow – a globe-trotter, as he said – and needed to be free again. He told us that as soon as he'd saved enough money, he intended to cross Africa on a horse.

I also discovered that he'd been a student but had failed his final exams. Now he trotted the globe, going everywhere, doing everything. He had written articles about some of his exploits and pasted them into a large album, which he showed to me after we'd eaten our meal.

But I was horrified later when he presented me with the bill. It was enormous.

True, we had been grateful for his aid with the bikes, but I did not see why we should be expected to help finance his projected African expedition as a reward. It was the last straw at the end of a difficult day. I disputed it with him, Agnes stood behind me to give some moral support.

Eventually, sighing, he reduced it by half.

24

TOWARDS RIMINI

'I wonder if our bikes will be at the station,' I said the following morning as we ate our breakfast in the Laplander's office-cum-dining-room. I was always just that little bit less optimistic and more sceptical than the other three.

'Of course they will be,' the Laplander assured me stoutly, his voice quite indignant that I should even doubt that they would be. 'Have no fear.' He was used to dealing with lazy officialdom, he told us.

He was right. After he'd driven us and our baggage to the station in his commandeered lorry, we were met immediately by a station official, who almost pushed the four of us into the office.

'Bicycles found!' he told us in English, smiling proudly.

But before he would let us be reunited with our four machines, I first had to pay out some money and sign for the bike which hadn't appeared on the form.

Then the official opened the door of the office, which led out into the street and '*Là*!' He made a flourish like a ringmaster at a circus. There, standing in a line, like horses waiting to be mounted, were our four missing bikes.

We loaded them, then clambered on, feeling rather embarrassed. It seemed that the porters had wheeled them out while we were inside the office, busy paying and signing the form. The entire staff turned out to clap and cheer as we rode off.

That day – at long last – we were cycling towards the blissful Adriatic.

At first it was very hot, but when we drew nearer the coast a cool wind blew inland from the sea. By now, not only Barbara but all of us were dreaming about the perfect campsite, set so romantically by the water's edge, an oasis, an idyllic image of beauty and tranquillity.

Yet, like so many dreams, it never quite became a reality. We merely continued on our tiring journey, which took us mile upon mile along a dusty, seemingly never-ending white road. The green rim of the sea was often just visible above the treetops – so near, yet so tantalisingly difficult to reach.

Then there was the disappointment when a jubilant Agnes led us off down a side-turning – beside which was a small board saying Campeggio di Conmiliti – and towards what she thought was a camping ground. It was a campsite all right, but a military one with enormous bell tents.

However, shortly after this embarrassing mistake, we found ourselves, to our surprise, on the sea front.

It was far from perfect and not at all the oasis of our dreams. As with so many of the seaside resorts in our own country, a multitude of people had arrived there before us. The roadway was lined with bungalows, villas, hotels and cafés. Nevertheless, it was our expedition's first proper view of the cool sea.

'Let's have a swim,' Esme suggested, dismounting, not waiting for us others to agree. She felt dusty and tired, as we all did.

So, leaving our cycles and baggage beside the roadway, we staggered over the sand dunes against a strong wind, which blew a silvery sand into our ears and hair. We found an empty, half blown-over tent to undress in. The water was quite rough – strong currents pulled us sideways along the beach – but it was wonderfully refreshing to wallow in its coolness after our hot ride. We felt like a party of dolphins, rolling over and over in the billows.

Then, after a sparse meal of bread and jam, eaten under one of the striped sails placed as windbreaks at intervals along the coast, we lazed in the sun. The Laplander had told Agnes that there was a hostel at Rimini, which was not far away.

'We'll spend the night there,' she suggested now.

'A few days, perhaps,' Barbara added, yawning. Although this beach wasn't up to what she had envisaged, it would have to do.

'A rest from cycling,' Esme agreed, stretching out languidly beside her.

It was so pleasant and relaxing just to lie there and bask that we forgot the time. Evening had crept up stealthily again, catching us unawares, when at last, dressed and ready, we cycled towards the outskirts of Rimini.

We now had to find the hostel.

Agnes, our leader once again, decided to try and practise some of her limited and recently-acquired Italian on a man about to cross the road, and ask him if he knew the whereabouts of the Albergo del Gioventu.

He didn't. Neither did his companion, who in turn, repeated the question to a young couple strolling by. Within a short while we were surrounded by a crowd of people.

One of them, a plump lady whose ample figure bulged through her tight black dress, was also wheeling a bicycle. When Agnes's request was repeated to her, she nodded and smiled kindly. Yes, she would take us there if we followed her.

So we did, although with some difficulty, for in spite of her size, she was a speedy cyclist and ignored policemen and traffic lights. At length, after a tiring chase, she stopped and pointed to a large, white, imposing building.

It was the International Grand Hotel.

'We've got exactly 500 lire in the secret purse,' I informed them; it was barely enough for a stay at a hostel.

'My back light's stopped working,' Barbara wailed.

'As usual, we've landed ourselves in a fix,' Esme added accusingly, as if she herself was in no way to blame.

It was poor Agnes as usual who got most of the reproaches. It was due to her bad Italian, we said, which the fat lady had obviously misunderstood. She was too sure of herself. And it was she who had insisted that the Laplander had said there was a hostel in Rimini. None of us others had heard him say this.

It was rather unjust. We tended to expect too much of her without doing enough ourselves. It was all our faults: we were too disorganised, too casual, too sure that we would always somehow land on our feet.

Barbara, Esme and I wandered off down the road dejectedly, leaving Agnes and the fat lady looking distressed.

We didn't get far.

Barbara's back light had attracted the attention of the policeman who we'd just swooped past during our wild chase. The traffic had now sufficiently abated for him to leave it to its own devices for a while and step off his round platform to tell Barbara off.

He did not get far. It did sometimes seem that a benevolent deity was overseeing our tour. For while the policeman was starting to harangue us, a well-dressed, middle-aged woman approached our group. A tall man, erect and soldierly, silent but interested, followed behind.

'What is wrong? I speak English,' she said.

Agnes, now recovered from our attacks, at once launched into an expressive account of our difficulties, accompanied by gestures and wide swoops of her long brown arms.

But the lady shook her head when she mentioned we were looking for a hostel.

'I do not know of any youth hostel here, although I believe there is a cheap place somewhere for Catholic girls.'

'But we're not Catholics,' I pointed out.

'No. Well, you can say you are. I don't suppose they would know.' She shrugged this objection aside.

'We have a tent,' Barbara put in. For some reason Agnes, in her long explanation, had omitted to mention this. It was our proof positive that we had our own accommodation and were not scroungers. All we needed was a small plot of land, a house nearby and a tap for drinking-water.

'A tent! They have a tent!' the woman exclaimed, turning to her husband. She spoke rapidly to him in Italian. He nodded in agreement.

'You can put your tent in our garden,' she told us. 'It will be all right. Follow us.'

So we did, along the sea front, then down two steps into the front garden of a large house. Its grounds lay behind a wall and an iron gate, but it was difficult to say where the beach ended and the garden began. Only clumps of straggly grass had managed to grow between the silvery-brown ridges.

'If you put your tent there, you will have a good view of the sea,' the *signora* told us.

While we were erecting it, her son, Bruno, a good-looking boy of about twenty, came out of the house to see what was going on. He had the same sort of impatient temperament as the globe-trotting Laplander. When he saw Agnes and Esme struggling to get their wobbly tent-pole in position, he pushed them aside, then remade the splint, using a new piece of wood and some string he found in his mother's kitchen.

By then, many people had gathered round to watch. From them we discovered that the house was not a private one but a pensione, and that the signora, her husband and her son were only guests here. They had rented the ground floor for their holiday. Somehow she had managed to square our presence with the proprietor.

Bruno did not think the position chosen by his mother was a very good one. He made Agnes and Esme take down the tent they had started to erect and re-erect it in a corner of the back garden, where the ground was harder for pegs and where it would be sheltered by a wall.

Signora Rivetta was as active and bustling as her lively son. No sooner had the tent been put up than we found ourselves being shepherded into the kitchen for a meal. Her husband, a retired Colonel, took some wine out of a cupboard and we each drank a glass to commemorate our arrival.

25

CAMPSITE BY THE SEA

The people at Rimini proved to be very friendly.

The next morning while we were breakfasting on the little patio beyond the kitchen, who should we see but yesterday's fat lady. Only now she no longer had her bicycle but was wearing her swimsuit, which made her bulges seem even larger.

'*Buongiorno, signore,*' she called out to us, smiling. Then, seeing that we were happily settled, she waved and went down to the sea for her swim.

Yesterday's policeman also looked through the iron gates to shout his greetings, no trace of anger left on his friendly face.

Next Signora Rivetta came out of the kitchen and suggested that we stay another day.

'You can do your washing,' she told us. We surely needed to. The dust on the roads had made both us and our clothes filthy.

So we did it that morning, using a tub she lent us. But we found it too hot to work for long without becoming exhausted. Esme and I retired to our beds inside the tent.

After Barbara and Agnes had finished washing, they forced themselves to stagger over to the beach. However, they were not allowed much time to stretch themselves out and rest. Two guests from the *pensione* insisted on taking them off in their old car to visit the famous castle of Francesca da Rimini.

And this was not to be the end of their sightseeing. When they returned at about six, they found Bruno waiting. He had already shepherded Esme and me out of our tent and lined up the four bikes against the *pensione* wall. He had an old English guidebook, which his mother had unearthed, tucked under one arm.

'I am taking you on a tour of Rimini,' he informed us briskly.

And it was a real Italian cycle ride. Bruno, impatient and fiery, liked to ride very fast. It was as much as Agnes, let alone I, could do to keep up with him. Barbara and Esme were soon left far behind.

He refused to stop for anything or anyone. When we arrived at the level crossing, where the red and white barrier was down, he shouted '*Ecco! Ecco!*' and it was underneath and on.

After we had chased him the wrong way down one-way streets, past traffic lights and policemen, swerving crazily to avoid cars, he eventually drew up beside the large gateway built by the Emperor Augustus.

I was the first to reach him. My reward, if you can call it that, was to be given the guidebook to read aloud to the others when they arrived.

Once we had digested this information, we were off once more. This time to the church of Rimini, built by the Roman Emperor Sigismondo, to commemorate his love for Isotta.

He told us to place our bikes inside the church, although a notice forbade it, and led us through its cool and beautiful interior. Unfortunately, the guidebook was too old to be of much use. Two world wars had taken place since it was written. After the last war, sculptors and artists from all over Italy had tried to put this 'Humpty Dumpty' together again, but many of the art treasures referred to were no longer there.

Even so, Bruno insisted that I read aloud before we entered each chapel. It did not matter that there was a service in progress and that only Bruno with his mischievous brown eyes was listening.

After the church, he took us to the old Roman bridge, said to be indestructible because its builder was reputed to have been helped by the devil. This was a foolish old superstition, perhaps, but it was the only bridge left standing in Rimini after the last war.

From here, we rode off to the new part of the town and Bruno's favourite, 'the garage of ships'. He was beginning to pick up and make his own version of the English language.

The sea front, newly built, was laid out with gardens of colourful and sweet-smelling flowers. Tall lights beside the road made the moonlight superfluous. Out at sea, the bright beam from a lighthouse cut a path through the water. We paid a brief visit to Bruno's yachting club, where he showed us a picture of his boat on the wall.

This marked the end of the tour. From here, we were whisked along the front to the *pensione*. Bruno had done his duty by us. It was time for a meal and we were ravenous.

'Why not spend some of your holidays here?' Signora Rivetta suggested to us as we sat in the sandy garden the following morning. 'It is so pleasant by the sea. And you will be quite safe.'

Her husband nodded in agreement. Although he spoke very little – his face was usually hidden behind some paper or other – we had the impression that he followed what went on quite closely. Most of the time he agreed with his wife who, in turn, was dominated by the mercurial Bruno, a likeable boy in spite of his unpredictability and quick changes of mood.

Both Esme and I found him attractive, but not enough to quarrel over. Bruno showed his impartiality by directing his attentions equally between us. Although we would have liked to stay longer, it was really a question of finances, as I well knew. If we stayed here more than a few days, we would have to miss out on other places we had planned to visit.

Agnes was particularly set on our going to Florence because she knew that the International Camping Rally was being held there that year. We other three suspected that she probably wanted to ride in triumph on her bike to show the people there what we'd achieved to date. We felt that as she'd provided all the equipment and know-how for the tour, we shouldn't deprive her of this honour. Barbara, our artist and art lover, wanted to visit Florence, too. Also Spain. Especially Spain, she said. There was also the challenge of doing what we'd said we'd do. We had said we would visit seven countries, so seven countries we'd visit. Or bust!

We tried to put some of this into words for the signora, who listened half smiling while fanning herself with a paper handkerchief. Then she suddenly remembered a friend she had at Forli, a town which lay on our route towards Florence.

'He is a charming young lawyer, very eligible,' she remarked, eyeing Esme, to whom she'd taken a fancy – especially when she discovered that she had a half-Italian mother. Perhaps she saw Esme as a possible candidate for an Italian man's wife. Not where her own son Bruno was concerned – Esme would have been too placid for him. Anyway, Bruno was still a student and had some years ahead of him, studying law at Rome University.

'I'm sure you'll like him – he's so sensible and reliable,' she added.

Bruno had to get out a map and arrange the best route for us. Then the *signora* wrote a note in her sprawling handwriting, put it in an envelope on which she wrote his name and address and gave it to Agnes for safe keeping.

26

THE LITTLE HOUSE

We arrived at Forli the following day, sticky, dusty and dishevelled.

We had left Rimini rather later than we'd intended for we'd decided to iron our clothes in the kitchen before we left. Many of the guests in the *pensione*, who'd already said goodbye before they went down to the beach, returned to find us still packing. My last memory of Bruno was his laughing face shouting to us through the window of the kitchen, '*Arrivederci! Buon viaggio!*' before he went off to his yachting club.

The sun had been overbearingly hot when we cycled out of Rimini. We made sure we waved to the fat lady, on her bicycle again, and to the policeman on his round platform, conducting the traffic, or so it seemed. He appeared to have forgotten or forgiven us for yesterday's wild chase after Bruno.

On the advice of the *signora*, who had told us that we were quite mad to cycle at such a time of day, we had tied scarves round our necks to protect the tops of our spines. Then, with Agnes leading, we had tried to keep close to the side of the road, within the shade of the trees.

When we reached Forli, Agnes – unable to read the signora's spidery address on the envelope – gave the note to a passing man. He interpreted it quite easily, and obligingly guided us through the town to a cool, narrow street, shaded by lofty buildings. Our appearance and overloaded machines attracted many curious stares.

The *signora* had already phoned, as she had promised she would do. Dr Gustavo Cammelli, a tall, dark, bespectacled man with a serious air, was standing waiting outside one of the high stone buildings.

He spoke little English and was obviously embarrassed at suddenly having four girls imposed upon him. After he had glanced at our dishevelment with some distaste – he himself was scrupulously dressed – and taken the note, he politely showed the four of us into the house, then into the bathroom.

Later, when we were cleaned and tidied and once more in his cool hall, he explained haltingly that he was a bachelor and that his house was too small for so many.

'I will take you to friends. They also live in Forlì,' he told us.

These friends lived in a pleasant street lined with pink, flowery-headed saplings in a suburb on the other side of the town. Here it was spacious. The villas, which had gardens in front, stood well back from the road. Fig trees and vines clung to their white stone walls.

We stopped outside the largest one of these. Gustavo's friend was a major, a burly man with a fierce, military-style moustache. He appeared at the doorway almost immediately Gustavo rang the jangling bell.

Thankfully, he was not as intimidating as he appeared at first sight. After he had greeted us very courteously, he led us, with Gustavo following, down a side lane and into a concrete yard, which lay beyond his house. He waved an arm expansively as if to suggest we pitch our tent there.

It seemed very strange to us that he, an army man, did not understand about pegs being unable to penetrate hard surfaces. Perhaps he had not realised that we had a tent. Agnes pulled a spindly, now rather out of shape tent peg from a bag, to demonstrate that it could not possibly penetrate the ground here.

'*Si, si*,' the Major nodded impatiently. It seemed that he had been meaning something quite different.

A small stone house stood at the end of the yard, empty except for a tap. He explained that it was eventually to be turned into a laboratory for his son, now away, who was a chemist. Meanwhile, we could use it instead of our tent.

His wife, a gentle-faced woman, appeared unobtrusively out of the back of the house. She shook her head when she looked at the stone floor, which she indicated would be too hard for our backs. She gave instructions to a young servant girl behind her that mattresses should be brought out.

More was yet to come. To our amazement, after the mattresses had appeared, a round, green table and chairs were carried into the concrete yard. Then – we almost rubbed our eyes to see if we were still awake – came food. There were plates of peaches and melon slices, bread, ham and a bottle of wine. This last the Major himself brought up from his cellar.

We felt as if we'd walked into a fairy story. The small house with a roof shaped like a pointed witch's hat, along with the large palm trees and their long sweeping comb leaves on guard beside the door, had an enchanted air. Fig, apple and pear trees and grapevines grew round most of the yard, forming a natural wall. Sweet-smelling jasmine and red and white carnations in pots grew within this charmed circle.

The Major brought out a standard lamp – it was now dusk – to illuminate our meal before he and his wife disappeared into the house, leaving us to eat this banquet in peace. Then Gustavo, relieved now his duty was done, rode off on his bike.

But this part of the story was only just beginning.

'Good evening, *signore*.'

We looked up from our feast in surprise to see a slim, dark young man swing one leg over the low wall behind the foliage. He walked over to our table and bowed. 'I am Filippo.'

Then he seated himself in a vacant chair, crossing one elegant leg over the other. 'I am to be your guide, philosopher and friend during your stay at Forli.'

Unlike the dignified Gustavo, he was not at all embarrassed by this role. His large, bright brown eyes shone as he spoke. He looked at each of us in turn as if at that moment she was the most important person in the world for him.

His English was very fluent for he taught it in a nearby school. Because of this skill, he told us, he would be able to explain many things we might have found puzzling about Italy. 'I have visited England. I understand how you think. I have things in proportion.'

'The roads,' Agnes said. She still had that day's ride fresh in her mind. 'The hooting, the wild driving...'

'Ah, yes,' he interrupted. 'The Italians are very individualistic. They like to break the law, although paradoxically, many of them study it. There are probably more lawyers in Italy per head than in any other country in the world. But Italian law is very intricate. In fact, it is impossible. So it has become a game – part of our temperament, our way of life – to break it.'

He continued to talk to us about Italy as we ate. There was the grinding poverty, their hatred of the Germans and all things German, the lack of proper education, and women...

His eyes grew dreamy as he expanded on this last subject. 'When a woman speaks to a man you may have noticed it takes him some time to answer. This is not because he has no manners. He has first to look at her and admire.'

When we had finally finished this meal, Filippo, or Philip, as he told us to call him, asked what we would like to do next.

'I am your servant, your genie of the lamp. I am yours to command.'

We decided unanimously that we'd like to explore Forli.

Later, as we strolled through the town with him, we unexpectedly bumped into Gustavo, who said he was just on his way to visit us. He and Filippo had not met before although they knew of each other through the Major, and had, in fact, often passed each other in the street without knowing who the other one was.

While they were discussing this, Filippo was hailed by two of his fellow teachers. Like him, they were both fairly young. One was small, with a humorous, lively face: the other tall, thin, and with drooping, scholarly shoulders. They joined the party, bringing the number of our group up to eight.

But the roadside was no place for talking. Quite soon, we all strolled into one of the brightly-lit cafés and sat down on a balcony, which overlooked the crowded street below.

I found myself next to Filippo who, in spite of his play-acting and exaggerated gallantries, I was beginning to like. As there was an escort for each of us, there were no rivalries. Gustavo, as Signora Rivetta had hoped, was very taken with Esme, especially now she was cleaner and was wearing a freshly-laundered dress. Agnes had Felice, the tall, stooping schoolmaster, and Barbara had Benito, the small, humorous one.

Unfortunately, we did not have much time to get to know each other. On the stroke of eleven, the door of the balcony opened behind us and there stood the Major. He rapped out a few short sharp sentences to Filippo, who jumped to his feet, standing to attention as he listened. Then the Major withdrew, abruptly slamming the door behind him.

'I have to return you at once. The Major wishes to lock up his house and go to bed,' Filippo spoke regretfully, suggesting that it was the last thing in the world he wanted to do.

So the eight of us walked slowly back through the town.

To amuse our young escorts, Agnes took this opportunity to tell them about our escapade with the singer in Austria. This brought the retort from Filippo that the honour of Italy demanded that they follow the Austrian singer's romantic example.

'In Italy to say that a man is a no good lover is the greatest insult you can offer him.'

However, there was little chance of their proving anything in the Major's house. When we arrived back there, we found him standing in the doorway, the key in his hand, like an old-fashioned Victorian father. It did not matter that we had travelled all through Europe on our own. While we were in his house – or garden – we were under his protection. Our escorts had to bid us goodbye very decorously, with much shaking of hands and clicking of heels, before they departed.

We retired to the little house and settled down to sleep on the mattresses.

'We must wake early tomorrow morning,' Agnes told us firmly. 'It'll take us at least two days to get to Florence, even if we leave before midday.'

We fell asleep quickly, glad of the mattresses and hoping that we would not oversleep.

27

ANOTHER SETBACK

So much for our good intentions and plans.

When we awoke the following morning it was pouring with rain outside. Our bicycles, which we'd left in the yard, were dripping wet. The round, green table held an ever-expanding puddle in its centre, as did the chairs round it.

'It's too wet to shop, even,' Barbara moaned, wishing that we hadn't eaten up all of yesterday's banquet.

There was nothing we could do but sit it out hungrily and wait for the rain to ease off. The little house was no longer enchanted. Bare stone walls and high barred windows made it seem more like a prison cell than a fairy-tale building. Our two guards, the large palm trees, dripped wretchedly outside.

Still, even though we were imprisoned inside it, we did have a few visitors to share our sentence temporarily. In fact, eventually, we began to feel that we were holding court in the little house.

First came our knight Filippo on his bicycle and carrying, most usefully, an enormous black umbrella. Holding this aloft, he most gallantly escorted us each in turn to the gabinetto (toilet) without in any way indicating that this was an unusual thing to do. Then he handed me the umbrella and Barbara and I went off shopping together. The man in the shop at the end of the road seemed to know all about our long ride. He kept pointing to our legs and asking if we felt tired. Then he served us some food as if he thought we were champions and needed good feeding, and bowed us both out of the shop.

Filippo stayed to talk to us while we ate our breakfast later in the little house. He looked quite dapper sitting on the one chair we'd brought in last night to hang our clothes on. By then, everything we weren't wearing was on the floor and mixed up with the bags, blankets and food, all in one glorious jumble and muddle.

Filippo told us more about Italy, especially what it was like to have been there during the war at the time of Mussolini and fascism.

'It was very difficult at school to be allowed to learn English. You cannot understand how it feels to live under a dictator.'

Perhaps talking to us stirred bitter memories. Also the dampness and rain were depressing. Irritated, he suddenly jumped up, almost knocking the chair over. 'I have to give a lesson.' He grabbed his umbrella and was off, barely even bothering to say goodbye, or whether he would be coming back before we left.

He hadn't been long gone before we had our next visitor, Gustavo, also under an umbrella. And he was carrying Esme's powder compact, which she hadn't yet missed, neatly wrapped in brown paper and tied with string. Apparently she had left it behind in his bathroom.

He sat on Filippo's empty chair – the four of us were squatting on the mattresses – and stared around in what can only be described as disgust at our squalor. Filippo had told me last night that Gustavo was quite well off and liked comfort. His manner was stiff and disapproving although his glance did linger a bit in Esme's direction. He didn't stay long. It was probably a duty call.

Next came the Major's wife. She was a sweet lady. She brought us a pile of biscuits, shaped like fish, on a Japanese dish. Then she sat down with us; not on the chair like Filippo and Gustavo, but on one of the mattresses, amongst the jumble.

She talked to us as if she were really interested in us and wanted to know what we were like. She explained through Esme, whose dormant Italian was now coming unexpectedly to life, then using a dictionary and signs, that she and the Major only lived on one floor of the villa – otherwise she would have put the four of us up in her house.

But the weather remained cold and damp. It was not until about four o'clock that the rain actually stopped and a watery sun appeared through the clouds. Agnes decided that we might consider starting on our journey again.

After we'd dried our bikes and loaded them with our baggage and tent, the Major's wife asked us to wait, saying she would like to take a photo of us before we left.

The Major, who'd now appeared, agreed that he'd like this record of our visit. But first he wanted to show us something. He pointed out a signature – JOHNNY, HUDDERSFIELD – scribbled on one of the outside walls of the little house. It seemed that we were not the only ones who'd used it for shelter. It had also harboured some English soldiers during the war.

At last, when we were ready to pose beside our machines and the Major, Gustavo turned up again. He had come to say goodbye for the last time. He stood next to Esme, resting his arm on one of her shoulders. We all smiled dutifully. The Major's wife pressed the button on her old-fashioned box camera.

Most amazingly, at the same moment there was a loud report. Esme screamed. Gustavo dropped his arm.

Had somebody fired a shot?

Barbara's back tyre had burst.

She was horror-stricken, as we all were when we discovered what had happened. It was a real calamity. It was now about five o'clock and the tyre had split in such a way that we could not possibly mend it ourselves.

We would have to buy another – that was if we had enough money. And it was quite likely that they didn't make that kind of tyre in Italy. Agnes was almost sure they didn't.

'Oh, why didn't we bring a spare?' she groaned, although goodness knows where we could have carried it if we had.

Again it looked very likely that one member of the party would have to finish the tour by train.

However, it was now that the dignified Gustavo came into his own and showed his true worth. Signora Rivetta had been quite right about his being sensible and reliable.

He now took charge of the situation, bidding the four of us to stop talking and wheeling around in despair and to listen to him. Things might not be quite as bad as we thought. It so happened he knew of a good mechanic who had a shop in Forli and might be able to help us.

Gustavo wasn't promising anything as he pushed our damaged bike out of the yard with us following behind. We feared but had to know the worst, and as soon as possible.

And miracles! Fate really was on our side. Our tour really must have been protected by some kindly god.

The man in the shop, who knew Gustavo well, did have a tyre of the right size among his collection. Also, and probably because Gustavo was with us, he agreed not to charge too much. The only difficulty was that he had other work to do: he couldn't start on our job right away. This meant we couldn't leave Forli that day. We would have to spend another night in the little house.

After this had been settled, Gustavo, who seemed much less stiff and formal now that we knew him better, invited us four to have supper with him in a restaurant nearby.

'I would like to watch you eat spaghetti,' he added, smiling shyly. His English had improved enormously in the last hour.

We did not find him such good company as Filippo. He could not tell us so many interesting things about Italy, nor even Forli for that matter.

'I am not a scholar of religion and history,' he told me, when I was collecting information for my diary.

'Nor a botanist,' he added to Agnes when she asked him the names of plants we passed in the street.

'But I am a man of action,' he assured us proudly. Then with great gusto he described the part he had played in the last election, especially how he had fought with the communists in the street.

'Although I was taken to hospital, I managed to break two of my opponents' noses first,' he added with relish.

To our great delight, Filippo joined us later at the restaurant, also his two friends, Benito and Felice. But these three certainly didn't share Gustavo's fiery, almost fascist views on nationalism.

'Please do not let us talk about politics,' Filippo begged. 'It requires only two Italians to make a revolution,' he explained to me.

The Major had given instructions that we be returned home early because he didn't like having to stay up late. When our meal was over we strolled slowly back to the house. I walked ahead with Filippo. It wasn't long before he was discoursing on his favourite subject – women.

'You have probably noticed that there are not many about in this district,' he remarked to me. 'This is because many of the better-off ones go away to the sea in summer.'

Then, 'Italian women are very smart, even the poorest, because material is so cheap here and they can make their own clothes.

'Not in winter, though,' he added. 'They have to put on everything they have to keep warm. They resemble Eskimos. In spring they emerge again, like butterflies bursting out of their chrysalis.'

'What do they do with themselves?' I asked.

'They usually work indoors at home. There is much to do in the preparation of food. When they've finished, they meet their friends. They do not wish for any other sort of life.

'But we Italian men like you English girls because you're

so different. You're so free,' he continued enthusiastically. 'Even so, we don't really want our women to change,' he added quickly.

When we reached the Major's house, the Major was waiting outside as he had been on the previous evening. This time, probably because he knew us better, he was more like a twentieth century father. Our leave-takings from our companions were longer, less formal.

'Tomorrow we will escort you out of Forli,' Gustavo promised.

Agnes told our four escorts that she would give two blasts on the whistle in the morning when we were ready to leave our fairy-tale house.

28

TOWARDS FLORENCE

Agnes did not have to blow on the whistle the following day.

When we awoke, rain was falling in large drops in the yard outside. It did not last as long as on the previous day, though. By the time it had stopped and the sky had cleared sufficiently for us to trust it not to start again, both Filippo and Gustavo had arrived.

The two men now seemed to be firm friends and were referring to each other as 'my friend Gustavo' and 'my friend Filippo'.

The Major, who had told us that he was worried by the thought of four girls camping on their own in Italy, had written a letter of introduction for us. He told Agnes she should present it to an old friend of his who lived in a village on our way to Florence. It seemed that he was quite an important local man, a wealthy landowner, and that he would probably invite us to stay in his house. If not, he would certainly let us camp on any part of his large estate which he considered safe.

Eventually, we were ready to leave.

The Major, with truly sweet, old-world courtesy, presented each of us with one of his special carnations, while the signora, who was very emotional, was weeping.

It was midday. We met Felice and Benito at the end of the road – it was their school lunch-hour – and our small party cycled slowly out of Forli. Filippo rode in front with me, next came Gustavo with Esme, and the other four followed some distance behind.

Filippo put a warm hand on my back so that he could push me along, far ahead of the others.

'Tonight we will all cycle over to the address the Major has given you,' he promised. 'I know the place well. There's a good café near his estate where we can all eat and dance.'

The four men could not accompany us far out of the town as they all had to return to work. Still, it was only 'Arrivederci' for now: we would meet again soon – that evening, Filippo said, either at the house or the campsite.

It wasn't so hot now. The rain had moistened the air and we were cycling in the shade of the mountains. We felt we were in a very ancient land, whose meadows had been cultivated for centuries. Long ages had moulded their contours behind the tall sunflowers and fields of ripening corn. Our road was bound by cypresses, smothered in white shells – snails brought out by the dampness – and planes and firs.

We did halt very briefly at a café for a drink but it was too noisy and too crowded for us to want to stay there for long. So we continued on our journey, but stopped later in a field, which sloped downwards away from the road. Agnes undid a pannier and we spread our groundsheet out under the trees.

Oh, it was wonderful to relax in the sunshine and dreamily watch white clouds drift across the deep blue sky, or the antics of two thin goats climbing bushes to nibble leaves at the top. We dozed off, forgetting everyone, everything, even our assignation, letting the sun's gentle warmth caress our bodies into sleep.

It was Agnes, our indefatigable leader, also the only one of us who had a watch, who woke us at last.

'It's a quarter past five!' she shouted at us in dismay. 'We won't get anywhere near the Major's friend's house this evening unless we leave immediately. And you'll have to cycle REALLY hard.'

Even so, we couldn't be bothered to rush and collected ourselves very languidly. We felt dazed, half-asleep, as we started to cycle slowly on again towards the place where the Major's friend lived.

But we were never to arrive there. Again fate took a hand in our plans.

While Agnes, the most determined, was trying to force her way quickly along the now upward sloping road ahead of us other three, she was suddenly hailed by a brown-faced lorry driver leaning down from an enormous lorry.

'*Firenze?*' he called.

Firenze – Florence – our ultimate destination and still a very long way ahead. Agnes hesitated. It seemed too good an opportunity to miss.

'I have *tre amice*,' she held up three fingers, rather unnecessarily, as a perspiring Barbara, Esme and I – who he must have already passed – were nearly upon them.

'*Firenze? Firenze?*' he shouted at us impatiently.

'What shall we do?' Agnes asked us. 'Remember we'll have to cycle up and over mountains to Florence.' The Major and the four men had warned us about what lay ahead.

'I think we should accept the lift,' Barbara spoke first. Then Esme, only really lukewarm towards the dignified and stately Gustavo, yawned her agreement.

It was a democratic decision. I was probably only the really disappointed one. I had liked and been flattered by Filippo's obvious interest. It was usually Barbara who attracted men's attentions. And he had given me a lot of useful information for my diary. Agnes and Barbara had both liked Felice and Benito, but not so much that they would forego a lift over the mountains to Florence just to see them again for one evening.

So to Florence it was.

The driver and his mate, who appeared out of the other side of the lorry, climbed down and helped us heave our machines up into the back of the vehicle.

Neither of the men could speak any English but they were both very clearly amused by the idea of four girls trying to cycle over the Muraglione Pass. The driver held one arm up to indicate its steepness. Agnes did try to explain but couldn't make them understand that we had intended taking about two days, and then maybe a bus.

When we reached the highest village on the route, the driver and his mate exchanged places. It was a severe strain to drive for any length of time on such a narrow and apparently dangerous road. The way became even more precarious when we slowly descended the other side. Parts were still under construction and some of the white 'teeth' marking its edge were missing, as if a lorry or some such vehicle had crashed down into the valley.

And this had really happened, the driver indicated. Taking his hands off the wheel, he mimed a description of how a lorry had plunged to its destruction. Then he grinned, flashing his white teeth. Such a calamity could never happen while he was driving, he assured us.

When it was dark, the lorry stopped for a while at a wayside café. The two men climbed out and went inside, leaving us alone.

While we were waiting, two policemen, armed with revolvers, strolled slowly down the road to our parked vehicle. They glared at us so suspiciously that we thought that we had somehow unwittingly broken the law. We had. It was apparently illegal for lorry drivers to give lifts.

When the two drivers returned the policemen called them harshly to attention and an angry argument followed. They all shouted and gesticulated in the direction of the lorry.

'Smile but look sad so that they'll take pity on us,' Agnes urged. We did our best to comply, but naturally enough found it difficult to manipulate our faces to smile and look sad simultaneously.

Eventually, the two policemen shrugged their shoulders, swung round on their heels, and walked off down the road.

'*Polizia!*' One of the drivers spat scornfully into the gutter

– but only after the two policemen had turned the corner. They were also careful to switch off the light inside the vehicle, so that we passengers could not be seen, every time we passed through a town.

'*Dove?*' they asked when at last the lorry rumbled into the dark streets of Florence. '*Dove?*' Where did we wish to go?

We did not really have much idea. Agnes knew the International Camping Rally was being held somewhere in Florence at this time. She thought it would probably be in the park, but on which side of the city this was situated, or even its proper name, she didn't know.

While we were debating the best way to find it, Esme espied a car trailing a caravan behind with a GB number plate on it. The two sunburned occupants looked as if they might well be connected with an international camping holiday.

Barbara leaned out of the window to shout down at them in her loudest voice. 'I say there – do you know where the International Camping Rally is?'

If the driver was surprised at being addressed in English by a girl sitting with three others high above him in a large lorry, he did not show it. He merely replied flatly: 'No. We're just following the arrows.'

'Arrows?' Agnes exclaimed, mystified, before she jumped down to the ground with us three close behind. We pulled our machines out of the back, thanked the drivers most profusely for their help and kindness, then started to search the street for these mysterious signs.

Whether these arrows ever really existed we never did discover. While we were busy striking matches, scouring the highway for their marks, a motorcyclist drew up beside us and asked if we wanted the international campsite.

Then, as if just asking was sufficient, he was off through the town without bothering to wait for a reply, .

We chased after him, helter-skelter down narrow alleys, bumped over a bridge and into what appeared to be a vast, badly-lit park. Agnes, leading, could only just see his rear lamp bobbing ahead like a glowing red will-o-the-wisp.

When at last he stopped, we caught up to find ourselves outside the barrier of a camp.

Everywhere was noise and activity. Voices were shouting, music blaring, lights flashing, cars arriving, people walking, running, talking. Eventually, feeling bemused and bewildered, we found ourselves standing before a table, answering questions.

'You have come from England. How have you come?' a perspiring, shirt-sleeved man asked impatiently.

'By bike,' Agnes began proudly, but her triumph was short-lived. Before she had time to expand on this and start to tell the grand epic of our tour, we had our machines jerked out of our hands by four officious Frenchmen, whose self-appointed task was to help new arrivals. They escorted us firmly, if noisily, down a roadway towards the tents.

These appeared to be pitched in blocks by country. This was no tent town like we'd stayed at in Innsbruck. It was a truly international city of campers. We erected our tent in the British section, using a Yorkshireman's car head lamps for light. We had a brief meal – the remains of some sausages and peaches – and went to bed.

We had actually arrived. Somehow, miraculously – unbelievably – we were in Florence.

29

FLORENCE

We were awakened early the following morning by people talking and walking around us; car and caravan doors opening and shutting; motorbikes revving up – in fact, all the usual bustle and activity that takes place in a large camp.

The International Camping Rally was situated in the wooded part of the Cascine Park in Florence and gave campers from camping clubs around the world the chance to meet and enjoy their shared pastime together. As each country had its own section with a national flag flying above, it could be described as a sort of sylvan map of Europe. The nations could meet in the centre where improvised shops stood and where there were also showers, toilets and drinking-water taps. The overall plan was quite good: it was just in its details that things sometimes seemed to break down.

Agnes and I set off together to buy some bread, milk and eggs, leaving Barbara and Esme to tidy up and get things ready for breakfast. As the two of us walked down one wide path that criss-crossed the park, Agnes suddenly stopped in front of a large brown tent.

It was very square-looking, solid – if a flimsy tent could ever really be described as such – and certainly very English. Two wooden boxes stood either side of the open flap. But it wasn't these, nor the old car drawn up behind which caught Agnes's scanning attention. It was a patch, not quite the right colour, but near enough, neatly sewn on the left of the flap.

'My stitches!' Her pale eyebrows almost disappeared into her flaxen hair as she bent closer.

'It can't be.'

But it was!

Before she had time to make any more observations, her father himself emerged backwards through the tent doorway.

'Daddy! But why – how on earth did you get here?'

When her father had turned round and straightened himself, he was pleased, nay delighted to see his daughter, but not as surprised as she was to see him.

'You got my letter? I hoped you would.' He was smiling broadly.

Now, it turned out that he'd written to the Poste Restante at Innsbruck, telling her that he and her mother had decided to come abroad for their holidays this year and stay at the International Camping Rally in Florence. It was a last minute decision. Perhaps helping us prepare for our Grand Tour had stirred their appetite for foreign travel. However, Agnes hadn't received any mail at Innsbruck.

'Perhaps we arrived too soon,' I suggested. Unlikely that. 'Or the man at the Poste Restante got your name wrong.'

'Well, you got here all right. That's all that matters.'

Her mother, hearing our voices, suddenly came out from inside the tent. Relief and pleasure were plainly marked on her plump, homely face. Although by now she had probably schooled herself to be fairly philosophical about her family's varied activities, Agnes's particular one must have given her some qualms. At any rate, she must have felt very glad to see her eldest daughter again, safe and sound.

It was about then that Esme and Barbara, still ignorant about Agnes's reunion with her parents, unexpectedly came across Fra, one of Agnes' many cousins who they'd met before, at the water taps. Barbara told us she nearly dropped our water-bag in surprise. They both stared at her as if they were seeing a ghost.

'So you made it,' was Fra's smiling comment. Her parents were staying there too. 'We were wondering how you were getting on. How are the bikes? Any punctures?'

We were all very pleased to see some of Agnes's family again. It felt rather like coming home. Also, we knew our bikes would get a good overhaul by Agnes's father, who would know exactly what needed to be done. Our unexpected meeting at the camp was a big bonus and probably the luckiest that had yet happened on the tour.

The time we spent in Florence was happy and relaxed, like a family holiday, but with the added excitement of being in a foreign city.

Apart from resting, we were determined to see as much as we could. We drove to the Piazza della Signoria, where the government of medieval Florence had once met and which was still the city's centre, joining Agnes's parents to first eat refreshing ice-cream before we started on any expeditions.

As in Venice, I had bought a guidebook out of the communal purse, so was able to read something of its history and background to the others.

I deluged them with pieces of miscellaneous information, such as that Florence Nightingale was born in Florence, which was why she was given her first name – a most unusual name for a girl at that time. 'Florence' actually means 'well adorned', words well suited to this lovely city in which history oozes from every corner, piazza and alley.

At one time Florence's noble families, mostly of German descent, played the most important part in the city's affairs. They protected their positions by building very tall houses – these were towers sometimes as much as 182 feet high – and near to each other, so that they could easily be defended together. During their period of power there were almost 150 of these giant edifices. But later, when the merchants seized the city's rule, these houses were cut down to a mere 75 feet.

Only the Palazzo Vecchio where the commune (government) met, retained its old height. Although looking rather aloof and out of place in the Piazza della Signoria, it is supposed to symbolise the destruction of the highborn city of towers. Crowning it stand the lily and lion, emblems of the Florentine Republic.

The statues which crowded the loggia and piazza below resembled a gathering of white giants from afar. Many of them – such as David, Perseus carrying the head of Medusa, Hercules and Cacus, Judith and Holofernes – symbolised the fate of tyrants.

The success of the merchants encouraged the development of many small shops, also artisans. Florence became a centre for fashion, particularly accessories such as coloured stockings, buttons, shoes, belts and bags. There were no large factories. You could say that the city's prosperity was founded in the first place on the imagination and nimble fingers of its working people.

As bitter fighting had taken place along the banks of the river Arno during World War Two, much of the surrounding area had been devastated. Fortunately, the Ponte Vecchio, its famous old bridge, had been spared. Also, by now, its shops had been restored. These medieval buildings, an oasis amongst the widespread devastation either side of the river, were a collective symbol of the city's continuous vitality. Florentine crafts – filigree jewellery, lacework, purses and all kinds of embellished leather work – were displayed in the windows and counters inside.

From the bridge we walked past Florence's new ruins, and where much rebuilding was taking place, to the Pitti palace, the city's most imposing and monumental mansion and once the residence of Italy's royal family.

As this was closed, we roamed through the nearby Boboli gardens, which were created during the Renaissance and had taken about a hundred years to shape.

The criss-crossed paths were shaded by tall hedges, so we were continuously finding ourselves in little self-contained groves. Here classical statues were posed around ornate fountains, or gazed down loftily from niches cut in the hedges. The garden was laid out so cunningly up the hillside that however high we climbed, we could never see its overall pattern.

It was intensely hot: the shrubs and trees barely trembled in the static atmosphere. The garden lacked the natural freshness and variety of an English one. We saw no flowers – its beauty lay in its perfect symmetry and arrangement.

On another day, we visited the Uffizi gallery, housing one of Italy's most famous collections of art. Again it was an unbearably hot day, but the gallery's interior was one of the coolest places in Florence. So trailing up flights of stone steps, then down corridors crowded with statues and paintings, was actually quite enjoyable.

The early works of the first few rooms seemed garish and crude to us, as if the medieval artists had not quite mastered their brushes and paints. Later, as we moved through rooms devoted to the Renaissance period, the portraits and scenes came more subtly and skilfully to life. Barbara and I were especially delighted when we came across 'The Madonna of the Goldfinch' by Raphael, because a copy of it hung in our hall at home. It was like an unexpected meeting with an old friend.

Our favourite day was the drive up and around the surrounding Florentine hills with Agnes's father. In spite of the squash and the car's hard seats, it was a welcome change to do our travelling so effortlessly instead of having to win every inch of our journey with our legs.

The dry green hills arising out of the dust, trees clustering gracefully around the red-roofed, white-walled houses, churches and towers, might have been one long series of paintings as found in the Uffizi galleries. The countryside itself could have been shaped by artists, as in a sense it was. Most of the Florentine sculptors and painters who had grown up in the surrounding villages and towns of Tuscany must have been influenced by their environment. Meanwhile perhaps the other members of their families, endowed with humbler talents, put these into the construction of their homes and the planning of their fields, vineyards and olive groves.

Florence lay below, straddling the valley either side of the silvery winding Arno. Its most famous landmarks – the Palazzo Vecchio of the Piazza della Signoria and Giotto's tower beside the enormous flower-like dome of the Duomo (cathedral) – glowed above the rooftops in the sunlight.

We spent another day exploring the city on our own. Like the paths in the Boboli gardens, Florence's streets criss-cross each other in such a way that it was difficult to understand its plan while walking through it. If you looked upwards at some of the houses, you could sometimes see square holes, as if a brick had fallen out and not been replaced. However, these were really slots which had once held the beams from bridges between the houses. Thus the noble families could combine their forces without having to brave the hostile streets below. More peaceful reminders of the past were the many madonnas set up high in niches, especially above the shops.

In spite of the complexity of the streets, we found the Duomo fairly easily. It is impossible to walk through Florence for long without seeing part of the great strawberry-shaded dome appear at the end of some alley or street.

At first, Agnes, Esme and I sat outside while Barbara took photos, not far from the place where the poet Dante had once watched the craftsmen at work on the cathedral's construction. Although the cathedral and adjoining baptistry and *campanile* (tower) harmonised well, they were built at different times, while the whole edifice took something like 900 years to erect. For centuries, watching the cathedral grow very slowly must have been quite a popular way for people to spend their time.

The baptistry, said to be the oldest building in Florence and rebuilt at the beginning of the thirteenth century, was splendid, especially the magnificent doors which, according to our guidebook, were made by Ghilberti. The tower, designed by Giotto, was intended to exceed in grandeur anything ever made by the Greeks and Romans, and was probably the most beautiful part of the whole.

However, we found the interior of the actual cathedral surprisingly bare and austere, more like a meeting place, perhaps even an extension of the Piazza, which had held so many Florentine gatherings outside.

Travelling around with Agnes's parents in their car had made us temporarily forget the hazards of cycling on Italian roads. On our return to the campsite that evening, we took a different route back on our bikes. We were given a speedy reminder of the long and probably dangerous journey that still lay ahead.

There were no traffic lights at the crossroads, nor policemen, nor apparently any right of way. Maybe it was that everyone had equal rights of way – an example of real Florentine democracy at work. All that the wretched unprotected cyclist trying to cross there could do was to close their eyes, call upon their favourite saint for protection – and full speed ahead!

Barbara, Esme and Agnes, doing this, managed to pass through quite safely. It was I, ever curious, who opened my eyes in this maelstrom of whizzing cars, lorries and motorbikes ando was nearly cut down by a speeding car, only missing death by inches.

Our last evening in Florence coincided with the official opening of the camp. Campers were still arriving from different parts of Europe.

Much fighting had taken place in and around the Cascine Park, which bordered the Arno, during the war. There were numerous shell holes to be seen and bullet-scarred trees.

The surrounding destruction and poverty was reflected in the park's lack of amenities. Italy, through Mussolini, had chosen to support Germany in the war, which retarded her recovery. Although the war had ended in allied victory some six years ago there was still much deprivation here. Some things, such as the supply of electricity, were not yet working again properly. This made it difficult for people to find their way around properly at night. As poverty and crime usually go together, thieving was rife. Police on motorbikes and camp officials were continually patrolling the park.

By day, cicadas added their clicking to the general noisiness. At night, darting fireflies surrounded the tents with pinpoints of illumination. Birds screeching at each other from the trees often sounded like people being attacked and robbed, or even murdered.

According to reports, a bonfire was to take place. The various nations – French, Italian, German, English, Dutch, Portuguese, Belgian, to mention just some – emerged from their sections of the 'map'. Two Italian policemen, very smart in their black uniforms and standing on a raised dais, surreptitiously surveyed the crowd, making eyes at as many girls as they could manage.

After speeches by the President of the Camping Club, the Mayor of Florence and the commissioner of the local police, the flags of each nation were solemnly unfurled, one by one, while the relevant country's national anthem was played. Then the campers marched off behind their flags in solemn procession, watched by a vast and appreciative audience of Italians behind the entrance barriers.

For some reason, which we never discovered, the bonfire did not take place. Instead, and probably better, there was an exhibition of Florentine dancing on the stage, lit by dependable floodlights. We watched the dancers – men dressed entirely in black (breeches, coats and flat hats) and women in flowered dresses and lace-edged caps – who were silhouetted against the dark sky. All around us, practically every European language seemed to be spoken. Campers' city was a true Tower of Babel.

30

TOO MANY HELPERS

Agnes's parents were to spend a further two weeks in Florence and we could stay on with them if we wished.

In some ways it was quite an attractive idea. It would have been a nice rest, and we did discuss it. But there was still Spain – and France – on our itinerary to visit. To return to England with Agnes's parents would have been a very tame end to our expedition.

We did also consider going down to Rome for a few days, but decided that we wouldn't have enough money or time. So the final consensus was to continue on with the tour as planned. Our long rest at Florence had done us good and we had the added confidence of knowing that our bikes and equipment were in good order. The expedition, refurbished, was ready to be on its way again. Spain was our next destination, via France and the Mediterranean coast.

Before leaving Florence, however, we did receive some recognition for our cycle tour. We *were* the only campers who had actually arrived by bike. We had our pictures taken standing by our machines by a local Italian press photographer.

However, as I (the sceptical one) noticed, we were posed in front of a shop selling scarves and mementoes and we might have been helping to advertise their wares as well. We were first taken altogether; then Agnes, our leader, was photographed smiling proudly on her own. Barbara and I, the two cycling sisters, were taken together. The four of us were finally taken looking at the scarves, as if we were customers, considering which ones to buy.

We rose early on the day our tour started up again but there was so much to do and so many people to say goodbye to that we didn't leave until midday.

By then, it was extremely hot. Although the road from the Cascine Park was shaded by trees, the vast square beyond was unprotected from the sun. After riding round it, we were obliged to collapse into a wayside café, where Agnes accidentally ordered almond water. It tasted horrible.

'An inauspicious start!' Esme remarked prophetically.

Still, the surrounding countryside through which we next rode was very beautiful, even if the sun was shining in our eyes, which made it difficult for us to see it as well as we should.

Eventually Agnes, in front as usual, drew up at a dusty village which had a water pump in the centre. Because she was so fair – there was a real Scandinavian look about her – she suffered the most in this hot climate. Esme, though not so fair, also found it hard to bear sometimes. Barbara and I, both of us dark, came off best. Although we dared not risk drinking the pump water, it was a great relief just to splash our hands, faces and elbows in the coolness.

The following day, when we were making towards Pisa, proved to be a day of accidents.

As I, leading but dazed by the strong sunlight, pushed my way up a hill, I tried to pass a barrow of tar which was sticking out at an awkward angle at the same time as a double-trailer lorry rumbled by.

Because my baggage behind was wider than the front of my bike, I misjudged the space. The lorry tipped my panniers and I sailed – quite gracefully, considering – over the handlebars and into the road.

While I was lying there, too surprised to be annoyed, a passing cyclist shouted abuse at the barrow man, now emerging from a shop, for placing his vehicle in such a dangerous position.

The barrow man shook his fist indignantly and shouted back. It wasn't his fault that the *signorina* wasn't looking where she was going, I supposed he said. Pushing his barrow in front of him, he walked off past the cyclist, the two of them arguing fiercely and completely ignoring me, the unfortunate victim lying in the roadway.

Still, I wasn't much hurt. By the time the others had cycled up, I was on my feet again.

At Cascina, a shabby, dilapidated town, badly battered in the war, Esme came off after catching her front wheel in a tram line. Agnes looked round on hearing the crash and fell too, cutting her leg so badly that we had to visit a nearby *farmacia* to have it bandaged.

Pisa, which had old-fashioned horse-drawn carriages for carrying tourists, was too busy, industrialised and crowded for us to want to stay there long. We contented ourselves with picnicking on the grass not far from its famous leaning tower, four metres out of perpendicular. We felt too tired to bother to try and climb the 300 steps to the top.

As we could not find a youth hostel in the town, nor did there seem to be a campsite, we camped near a shop where we bought our evening's food. Agnes tried out her newly-acquired Italian on a sleepy-eyed man inside, who we took to be the husband of the woman serving behind the counter. He suggested we camp in the orchard behind the shop.

As it was already crowded with apple, pear and fig trees, there wasn't much room for us. The man gave us some straw and sunflower stems, which Agnes heaped across the ruts. Barbara, looking rather like a Roman goddess, held our candle aloft to help us see what we were doing.

The next day, at long last, we were riding towards the Mediterranean coast.

At first, the roadside was wooded with pine and plane trees growing higgledy-piggledy in the sandy soil, then came camellias and plane trees, planted alternately, giving a sort of symmetrical elegance to the rest of the route.

I changed some money at Viareggio and we continued on our ride, now along the wide sea front. Here it was cooler, so cycling was less arduous. We saw a crocodile of children from an orphanage, the girls dressed in pink and the boys in blue. All were topped by round white hats. They were accompanied by a nun in long, flowing robes. Her white head-dress billowed out before her like the sails on a ship.

A crossing guard, carrying a red flag, held up the traffic for them to pass. The nun rang a tinkling little bell when it was safe for the children to cross the road. However, one impatient cyclist, ignoring the bell and the red flag, rode through the crocodile, scattering the children. The crossing guard was so angry that he chased the cyclist down the road. On catching him, he beat him over the head with the red flag.

That evening, we pitched our tent on a patch of land on the sea front, between pines and gorse bushes, not far from a caravan, whose friendly French occupants warned us to beware of marauding gypsies – there were apparently quite a number in the area – who would steal anything they could lay their hands on. They also told us that there was a good campsite at La Spezia, which lay on our route and from whose height there was a splendid view of the sea.

It was the thought of this idyllic place that lured us on again and kept us going the following day. We were obliged to leave the coast for a while and ride inland again, back once more into the hot dust of the noisy highway.

We had our reward later that afternoon when we were perspiring and dusty, too tired to talk even, especially after climbing a particularly steep hill. We turned a corner and emerged to look down on what seemed a blessed image.

Far below lay the bay – a cool, distant blue. Out at sea, situated on a rocky promontory, was the fortress of Lerici, now a youth hostel.

'The campsite must be on the other promontory.' Agnes compared its position with the cross the French caravanners had made on our map. 'We should be there before dusk if we don't have a rest.'

We others did not need much persuasion. It would be downhill, then along the coast. Soon we were speeding past olive trees, cypresses and vines down towards the houses and welcoming water.

We sped through the streets of Lerici quickly and did not linger long in the waterfront gardens. Even so, evening had arrived – the sky was flushed pink and the sun dipped gracefully into a gently greying sea – when we finally took a road to the right, which led away from the water and up the cliff side.

Agnes, unsure of the way in the dusk, asked a passing man for the direction of the campsite.

'*Sinistra, sinistra,*' he replied emphatically, pointing up a sloping path.

So we went left, struggling over the stones, pushing and pulling our heavy bikes. As we climbed slowly, it grew darker and the noises of the town gradually died away.

We were all listening keenly for the sounds of an active campsite but there seemed to be no human noise about up here. The myriad glittering lights of the town now lay far below. We could only hear the gentle brushing of the sea over the shingle and the ceaseless chirping of the cicadas.

'Where shall we camp?' Barbara asked at last. Agnes, undecided, had paused to rest.

'Let me explore,' I suggested, feeling suddenly brave. After taking a path round a rock, I found myself on a wide plateau, overlooking the sea. Was that tall pole part of a tent, I wondered, and the dimly distant moving shapes campers?

Alas, on closer inspection, I discovered that the pole was the outline of a goal post. I was standing on a football pitch. The moving shapes were merely sheep, nibbling at shrubs. They stared curiously at me as I bent down to feel the ground. It was as hard as concrete.

Disappointed, I rejoined the other three, who were still undecided as to what to do.

Agnes then suggested that she and I explore a bit more while Barbara and Esme guarded the bikes. She hadn't forgotten the French couple's warning about gypsies.

We had not got far down the other side of the cliff when I saw a man approach carrying a spade, rather like a gun, against one shoulder.

We both suspected that we had accidentally come to the wrong place. Maybe we'd taken the wrong path up the cliff. The first man must have misunderstood Agnes's question. She decided to ask this other man where the site was.

Here, he indicated to our great surprise, putting down his spade. Here, by the sea. He waved a bony hand all around. Only tonight, it seemed by chance, we were the only campers. Usually there were many campers – '*Inglesi, Francesi, Olandesi...*'

Agnes found it difficult to believe him. 'The ground's too hard.' She kicked at it angrily with her foot.

The man shrugged. We could believe him or not as we wished. He seemed to be telling the truth. He walked off leaving us to argue it out between ourselves.

While the two of us were discussing the advantages and disadvantages of sleeping on the ground beneath the open sky, we suddenly heard Barbara blowing on the whistle. Since the gondolier episode, she had continued to wear it round her neck.

'I say, you others...' These words, although purposefully laconic, were spoken with a suspicious tremble.

'Gypsies!' I exclaimed, remembering the warning.

We two hurried back along the path to the clifftop.

However, it was not the gypsies who had sneaked up furtively to steal our few shabby possessions. Barbara and Esme, who we'd left alone to guard the bikes, were now surrounded by a crowd of would-be helpers – a swarm of jostling, gesticulating, jabbering men.

Before Agnes and I had time to say anything, we found ourselves part of this busy, excited throng. Our machines, now lying on the grass, were seized, as was any other unattached baggage, and almost ourselves. Then we were escorted, nay bundled, back to the part of the cliff which Agnes and I had just left.

'Ooh!' Agnes groaned, sliding down on the groundsheet, which someone had managed to pull out of a pannier. She put her face in her hands, defeated. There was nothing, absolutely nothing, that she, nor any of us, could do to stop what was happening.

More and more men appeared, coming from nowhere, it seemed. It was almost as if they'd been hiding behind rocks and boulders, holes in the ground, or even out of the sea itself. They were making eyes, aiming probably to make love, fetching buckets of water, then knocking them over, talking, laughing and walking all over our baggage, which was now sprawled over the cliff.

'PUT UP THE TENT!' Barbara bawled suddenly, as if once inside we would be in some sort of fortress.

'If only we could stop them trying to do it,' Agnes moaned wretchedly.

For now, taking matters into their own hands, these men were trying to hammer our slender tent pegs into the rock-like ground, hopelessly bending them. The groundsheet lay awry as people sat on it, watching, or walked over it, helping. Everywhere was noise and confusion.

'We'll just have to sleep outside like we said,' I suggested, thinking it best perhaps to try and ignore what was happening.

'How can we?' Agnes shouted angrily, exasperated. One man nearby, overhearing and understanding, was pointing to the sky. Dark, tumbling clouds had almost blotted out the tiny edge of the moon, which swung over the sea. It would rain soon and it would rain hard.

Barbara was determined that the tent should go up. She shouted furiously at Agnes, who shouted even more furiously back.

Men grabbed at their arms, laughing, mock-restraining them when it seemed that the two of them might even come to blows.

Fortunately, both Esme and I kept our heads. It was while I was trying to calm down my agitated sister and Esme was doing the same with Agnes, that the crowd parted to let through a stockily built man.

'He speak English. He help.' One fellow touched my arm.

Our rescuer spoke two magic words, 'Follow me.'

So we did, Agnes and Barbara forgetting their argument and Esme and I grateful but curious. The matter seemed to have been taken out of our hands, and we were relieved to be constructively organised, even if it were only to allow us to escape from this noisy throng.

As we followed him, so we in turn were followed, and a long procession formed down the path. The people behind, pushing our bikes and carrying our luggage, escorted us boisterously to a small white house on the outskirts of a village.

A simple but dignified woman – the man's mother – stood waiting outside. She invited us indoors, where she politely indicated that we might stay a while.

Later, when the crowd had departed, disappearing back to the mysterious places from which they had come, she gave Barbara permission to cook our spaghetti on her stove. She made this up afresh with charcoal. Sparks flew all around us.

'You may sleep here, too,' Guilio, our rescuer, told us as we ate our meal in the narrow kitchen. Relieved and grateful, we spent that night in their best room, sprawled on our bedding over its tiled floor.

31

LA SPEZIA

We found Guilio a rather intriguing and slightly mysterious character.

He wasn't very dark for an Italian and he seemed much older than he looked. He was very quiet – almost withdrawn. Although he did not speak English often, we reckoned he must be quite good at it: Esme discovered a copy of *The Tempest* in our temporary bedroom.

The next morning after we had breakfasted in the narrow garden, shaded by dangling bunches of reddish-brown and green grapes, Guilio suddenly appeared in the doorway.

'My mother says you may stay here another day,' he told us politely. 'She suggests you do your washing,' he added, putting down the shopping basket he was carrying.

His mother, hearing his voice, came out of the house, nodding and smiling. Earlier that morning, she had kept pointing to our clothes and going through what must have been the motion of scrubbing. We hadn't understood what she meant. Sometimes the heat made us rather stupid.

She was a big woman, perhaps about fifty, but with the stately carriage of a queen. Her lined face was as tranquil as the surrounding hills. Nothing seemed to ruffle her: not even four strange females sleeping on the floor of her best room.

'Let's stay,' Esme put in quickly. She had taken quite a fancy to the taciturn Guilio. Anyway, it was a pleasant place. And we felt we could do with a rest again after the last few days' hard cycling. So the invitation was accepted. Once more, we were to do our washing in somebody's garden.

This time, though, there was no brook running by, no tap, nor wash tub. Water had to be fetched in an enormous bowl from a well in the roadway. Needless to say, we did not try to carry it on our heads like the village women we met, awaiting their turn round a well.

When Esme and I arrived there together, struggling to carry the heavy bowl between us, we were greeted politely before the women tried to question us about ourselves. But we felt too hot and tired to try to understand them. Unoffended, our questioners broke off, laughing and exclaiming at our not being able to understand such a simple language as Italian.

Guilio bred birds for a hobby. Cages of varying sizes hung along the front of the house. There were green and blue budgerigars, bright yellow canaries, linnets and a bright red cardinal.

At Esme's request, Guilio drew the red cardinal out of its cage, letting it perch blinking on his hand, while he affectionately rubbed its brilliant comb.

'Would you like a swim?' he asked, and put the bird back. 'All of you,' he added, for he had been looking at Esme.

A cool swim in the Mediterranean after our morning's exertions was too tempting an offer for any of us to turn down. About one hour later, when we'd all finished at the tub and our clothes were strung out across the small garden, drying in the warmth, we followed Guilio down to the sea.

On the way there and passing the scene of last night's drama, we were amazed to see a family of French campers unloading their gear from a ramshackle car.

'Their pegs must be of cast iron,' Agnes commented, almost unable to believe the evidence of her eyes.

Later, when we turned down a path and found ourselves near my football pitch, we saw a squad of men at work around the rocky sides, filling barrows with stones. Some of the men were probably the men of last night for they lowered their shovels and pick-axes to call out as we walked stiffly past.

Then, on seeing Guilio, they grinned, winked at each other and continued with their work.

After we had slithered down the cliff amongst gorse and sand to reach a pretty stretch of beach, surrounded by rocks, we undressed in a sort of Robinson Crusoe hut, which Guilio told us had been made by boys out of reeds. Then we plunged into the sea.

Guilio, for all his silence, must have been something of a local power. As we sunbathed on the rocks, although the beach now swarmed with men – there were no females about that we could see – not one of them approached our party.

However, our reticent rescuer had made his choice out of his harem of four. It was Esme, the placid, somewhat baby-faced member of the party, who seemed to have taken his fancy. After gently teasing her, tickling her feet with straw, he suddenly pulled the sunbathing girl to her feet.

'Come, I show you,' he said quite gaily and the two of them wandered off down the beach to explore its Mediterranean fauna. He showed her a dead locust amongst the driftwood, then a sea-urchin and a sponge.

On our way back to the house over the cliffs, he caught her a cicada. We were all fascinated to have a close-up of one of these insects whose clickings we had so often heard. It had strong transparent wings, a black and white armoured body and eyes like facets of diamonds – pinpoints of light surrounding a glittering bubble in the centre. Guilio explained that the sound was made by tiny drum-like plates at the base of its abdomen being vibrated by seemingly tireless muscles.

We were to spend one more night in Guilio's home before setting off again on our long journey.

32

GENOA

We would have liked to have stayed longer at La Spezia – it was such a pleasant place.

Esme even said she would like to live there, although we other three couldn't really imagine her carrying water-bowls on her head.

However, some of Guilio's relatives, already invited, turned up the following day for their annual holiday. There was Guilio's sister, her husband and two children; Francella, eight, and Pia, two and a half. We didn't fancy trying our tent pegs out again on the clifftop but their garden would have been too small for our tent. Also, we felt we would be in the way. We did wonder, though, how so many people could be squeezed into such a small house.

Guilio suggested that we make Genoa our next stop, then take the boat to Spain from there. Our plans were still fairly flexible, not yet properly worked out. The idea of travelling across the Mediterranean waters by boat appealed to us vastly. That's if it wouldn't be too expensive.

Guilio did not think it would be. He also suggested we take the train to Genoa as to cycle there would be a long and arduous journey.

'If you take a shorter time to arrive you will not have to spend so much on food for the journey,' he added wisely. We would also find Spain considerably cheaper than most other European countries at that time, he explained.

He guided us to the station on his motorbike, which he used a great deal in his job. He told us that his firm was expanding and that as he spoke English, he might even get a chance to visit London next year.

'You'll have to get in touch with us,' Agnes told him enthusiastically. He nodded, pleased, but I noticed that he only wrote down Esme's address.

He had already been to England twice before. On the second occasion, he'd been a waiter in a hotel, 'to improve my English', he told us. The time before that he'd been a prisoner of war.

We found the journey to Genoa most enjoyable. Our train travelled along the coast most of the way, sometimes passing through tunnels carved out of the cliffs as well as alongside the Mediterranean sea with its innumerable bays, inlets and tiny fishing villages.

Fortunately, when we arrived at Genoa, our bikes had too. Thank goodness for Guilio! Even the station officials seemed quite surprised. They said it was unusual procedure and made us wait a while before they let us collect them and ride off.

Genoa, with its magnificent seaport, palaces, ancient churches, gardens and orange groves spread out over the steep slopes of the Appenines, is probably best seen from the sea. For on closer inspection, this noble façade hides a network of mean, narrow streets, clumsily climbing the hillside.

The hostel was extraordinary to say the least. That we discovered it at all was only due to Agnes's peculiar instinct for sniffing out things that were hidden. There did not appear to be any signs anywhere to tell us where it was.

An arched doorway led into a cloistered passage. On one side were dilapidated buildings; on the other, statues, mostly headless or legless and armless, as if recently tossed out of an overcrowded museum. Tall masts and funnels screened the horizon behind.

Its entrance at the end of a passage was forbidding, its interior decrepit and decaying. Yet it had a certain seedy grandeur, a dilapidated elegance, as if it once might have been a minor palazzo.

Part of the office's ornate ceiling had collapsed onto the floor. The deterioration was probably the result of time, neglect and the ravages of war. The hostel was already full up.

But how did anyone know where it was? I asked the others, mystified.

Nevertheless we were allowed to stay. As used to be the case with certain London hospitals, there seemed to be an unwritten law that no one in need should ever be turned away.

After having slid about for two nights on our airbeds over Guilio's tiled floor, neither Barbara nor I were too fussy now where we slept. At least we would have a stable base to lie on. Even so, our dormitory was quite daunting. It was so crowded, dusty and hot that Esme nearly fainted. But when I tried to open its one window, to my horror, the whole frame came away in my hand.

We were awakened early the following morning by men walking around us. They had come to remove the beds borrowed to put up extra people. As most of them were still in use, the occupants had to be shaken and tipped out.

There was much for us to do that day: first to visit the bank, next buy some food, then find a boat that would take us to Barcelona. About this last, though, we were to be disappointed.

'There was a cargo boat calling at Spain on the way to South America,' the official at the information office told us. 'Unfortunately, it left four days ago. It sailed earlier than expected.'

'There must be another,' Barbara – who had set her heart on a boat trip – insisted, exasperated.

'Not for three weeks. A boat is not like a bus,' he replied stiffly, then added more helpfully: 'You might be able to get a boat from Marseilles.'

So it was to Marseilles in France that we went next.

The journey there from Genoa was quite an enjoyable one as the train hugged the coast for most of the way. The French Riviera lived up to its elegant, picturesque reputation, especially such well-known places as Monte Carlo, Nice and Cannes. But it proved a long ride and we did not arrive at Marseilles until about 10 p.m. By now, the four of us were fairly philosophical about the fate of our bikes. That they may or may not have arrived with us added an extra frisson, a spice of adventure, to the journey. Esme and I, the party's two cynics, declared they wouldn't be.

We were right. But the station official at Marseilles told us not to worry too much. Also, we should not blame French railways who, according to him, were very efficient. It would be the Italians who'd taken them off at the border.

'Perhaps they'll send them along tomorrow,' he said hopefully, shrugging. But who knew what the unpredictable Italians would or would not do.

The difficulty now, as on similar occasions, was that if we didn't have our bikes we couldn't carry the tent, which we left behind in the baggage department, meaning we'd have to spend another night at a hostel.

So, after obtaining the address of a hostel, we boarded a tram, which we were told would take us most of the way to this place. A woman on the tram who got off at the same stop as us, kindly walked with us to some park gates, behind which, she said, the hostel was situated.

If we had found Genoa ramshackle, decrepit and sordid, we found Marseilles even worse. At that particular time, it was probably one of the most wretched, unpleasant and disgusting places in the world.

By this stage it was quite dark. According to our guide, the hostel was not a building but tented accommodation. So, as we staggered over the grass with the baggage we'd had with us, we were not too surprised when we sighted figures humped around a bonfire, singing what sounded like sentimental German songs.

The tents became clearer as we approached the fire. We decided that the largest tent, which had two hurricane lamps standing outside, would be the best one at which to make our enquiries.

Inside sat a man, feet sprawled over the table in front of him. But before he had a chance to question us Agnes had launched into a long tale of woe in French, explaining that our bikes had not yet arrived at the station, which meant we had not been able to carry our tent. Would he let us stay the night at the camp?

'Impossible!' the man replied in English but in that particularly gleeful way in which certain shopkeepers had told people that they didn't have what they wanted during the war. It was as though they were delighted to disappoint you. I supposed they felt it gave them some sort of power.

'We have no room. Not an inch,' he added brutally, ignoring our crestfallen faces.

'We have sleeping bags.' Barbara pushed herself forward. She always maintained that Agnes's long speeches left out the most important piece of information.

'They have sleeping bags.' The man slapped his knee in simulated surprise to a tall youth who had entered the tent behind us. He had always thought, he told us, that the English never used sleeping bags, nor blankets, even, for that matter.

'You may sleep in a tent, but there are no beds left,' he told us unpleasantly and ordered the youth to take us to the dining tent.

This tent stank because a lidless bin stood just outside the doorway. Inside were some bikes, a long trestle table, benches, a stove, and two campbeds – already occupied by two snoring girls – taking up most of the space. Apparently it was an all-purpose tent, doubling up as a kitchen and dining room.

When I asked our guide to lend me his torch so that I could explore the ground more thoroughly, its beam revealed paper bags, empty cartons, old tins, peach stones and what looked like hundreds of scampering ants.

'It's impossible! We can't sleep here.'

Even Agnes was aghast. Barbara and Esme were speechless.

'Perhaps we can sleep in the open. Under the stars.' I suggested hopefully.

However, this idea turned out to be as impractical as it had at La Spezia. When I asked our guide where the toilet was, he stared at me as though I were crazy.

'*En plein air*,' he exclaimed, waving an arm expansively around, as if to show that here, in France, there was real freedom.

Well, that decided us! In spite of everything – the paper bags, empty cartons, old tins, peach stones and even the ants, we would have to sleep in the tent.

But our troubles were not yet over. While we were wandering dismally around, wondering exactly where to put our beds, the tent was suddenly invaded by the men from the bonfire. They were mostly German and Swiss students, who appeared delighted to see us. Under different circumstances we might have been delighted to see them, too. But not now.

Some good did come of this invasion, for they removed the bikes – which gave us more space for our sleeping bags. Then they thrust large mugs of newly-made mint tea into our hands.

'You're the first English we've yet met.' A German, wearing a guitar slung across one shoulder, sounded almost ecstatic.

'We've had French songs, German, Norwegian, Swiss, Italian, but no English ones. Will you teach us some English songs?'

Would we? There was an icy silence – in spite of their helpfulness moving the bikes and the mugs of mint tea. To have travelled all day only to end up at a place like this was almost as much as we could bear. Singing was the about the last thing we felt like doing.

'It's past twelve,' Agnes hissed.

'They're tired!' One of them said sympathetically. He must have been some sort of leader for when he clapped his hands authoritatively, they all trooped out of the tent.

'Tomorrow we will come again,' he promised before disappearing with the others.

Somehow we made up our beds, Barbara and I grumbling and swearing to the great amusement of the two French girls who had been awakened by the noise. Unfortunately, we two sisters were not philanthropic like Agnes, nor placid like Esme. Before we settled down to sleep, I surrounded our adjoining beds with scent, using a midget bottle of perfume kept at the bottom of my panniers, to counteract the smell from the dustbins.

PART FIVE

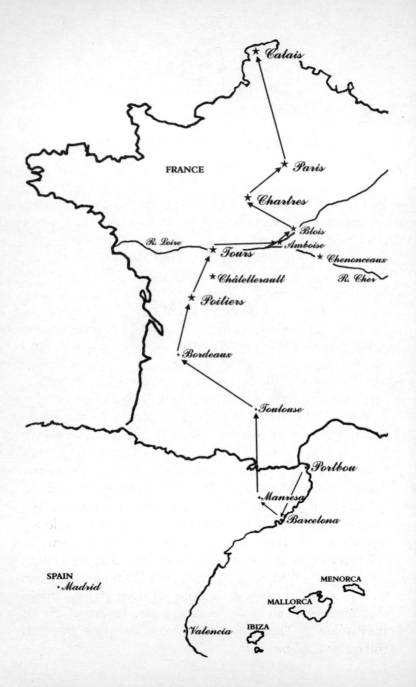

33

MARSEILLES AND TOWARDS SPAIN

Barbara and I, still angry the following day, kept up a running
commentary of disgust about the state of the tent and the
camp in general.

'*Ce n'est pas propre! Ce n'est pas propre!*' the two French girls
repeated mockingly.

We four left early and before the boys returned for their
singing lesson. But there was one compensation for this awful
place.

'We don't have to pay. What have we had that we could
possibly be asked to pay for?' I said.

Although Marseilles, founded by the Greeks about 600BC,
is one of France's most ancient cities, we found little there that
was interesting to see. Under the pretext of protecting public
health, the Germans had evacuated the densely-populated but
most picturesque area around the port and razed it in 1943.
Other bombings, both allied and German, had caused great
damage and many deaths. Although this had been rectified and
the city rebuilt, its architecture was mostly a product of the
nineteenth and twentieth centuries, a dull period for building.
To us it seemed a sprawling and rather characterless city.

When we emerged on it early, it was just waking up. Only a
few cafés were ready to serve customers. Yawning proprietors
were starting to open their shop shutters, pulling down
shabby awnings, and some putting out tables and chairs on
the pavements. There was little traffic on the roads and it was
still early-morning cold.

Later, while breakfasting around a chipped marble table, we saw quite a few sailors sipping coffee or playing cards. Gypsies, beggars and Algerians, in their long flowing robes, appeared. The Algerians, mostly traders, carried enormous baskets of bangles, bags, leather purses and trinkets. Some even had carpets draped over their arms.

As Agnes, such a friendly soul, felt the need to smile at them, our table was soon surrounded by these vendors. More used to rebuffs than friendliness, they could only interpret her apparent goodwill as a need for a bangle, a purse, or maybe a carpet.

'Cheap! Bargain! Beautiful! Beautiful!' they chanted, spreading out their rugs around them, although Agnes did her best to explain that we were '*très pauvre*', and that carpets were of no use to cycle-campers. When we finally left the café, we other three, in self-protection rather than hostility, had to take it in turns to watch her face. If there was the slightest suspicion of a smile emerging, we would jerk her arm and tell her to stop it.

No doubt at that time the poverty in Marseilles was appalling. We realised that it must be most demoralising to try to sell things to people which they don't want in order to eat. But we had little money ourselves. The problem was too big for us. If we'd given them anything, we would have been immediately surrounded. As it was, so many sly glances were cast in our direction that I felt very glad that the secret purse was hidden out of sight beneath my blouse.

We visited Thomas Cook's Travel Agency before going to the station. Here, we learned most disappointingly that there were no boats going to Barcelona from Marseilles. It seemed strange that the official at Genoa hadn't known this, but ship services were still sketchy and erratic, not yet having recovered properly from the effects of the war. If we really wanted to go to Spain, the best and quickest way there would be by train.

So it was to the railway station again, where we were to receive yet another disappointment. Our bikes had still not arrived.

'Let's go for a swim,' Agnes suggested as we sat dispiritedly on a wall. It was nearly midday and very hot again.

Our journey by tram to the beach was not a happy one. The conductor, as evil-faced a man as I'd ever yet seen, tried to make me pay our fares twice. He didn't succeed. Tight-fisted as always, I saw to that. But this unpleasant incident left us feeling limp and exhausted.

Worse was yet to come. When we arrived at the beach to which we'd been directed, words failed all of us. Even Agnes. Its state was disgusting. However, in spite of the litter-strewn shore and general filthiness, there were quite a few chairs and tables, shaded by striped umbrellas, spread out along the strand, while the grey-blue sea was crowded with bathers.

Agnes and Esme, very hot and less fussy than Barbara and me, joined them. Maybe it was their way of justifying spending money on the tram ride. Neither stayed in very long. Agnes even admitted to me afterwards that she had bumped into a dead dog.

Later while we were drinking coffee at a nearby café, a dark, ragged gypsy, suckling a tiny baby, sidled over to our table. On sitting down, she told us that she could tell fortunes. Barbara, on her left, was her first victim.

'I can see a tall, fair man – he's nearer than you think,' she said in a sort of broken English, still clutching the baby as she examined Barbara's palm. She also told Agnes and Esme that they would have to leave their homes and cross the sea in order to find their true loves.

She stopped, alas, when she came to me, because by that time, I, the treasurer, had run out of silver coins and knew it unlikely that she'd have change for a large note.

When we returned to the station about six o'clock, Agnes thought she saw our bikes hanging up behind the counter. But it must have been a mirage, wishful thinking, a figment of her imagination, or most probably, a result of the heat. The official there told us most regretfully that they had not yet come. As Agnes refused to believe this, he took the four of us on a tour of the station to prove it.

That evening, while eating our supper in a café opposite the station, we composed what we thought was a stiff letter to the Italian Customs Office. Fortunately, it was never posted. As we crossed the road to put it in the station letterbox, the official, seeing us again, came out smiling broadly to tell us that our machines had *just* arrived by train.

This wasn't quite the end of the matter. Our bikes still had to be cleared by French Customs before we could be allowed to take them out. And the French Customs Office was now closed!

Perhaps because we looked so pathetic and disappointed, but more likely because we had made ourselves such a nuisance that he wanted to get rid of us, the official opened the office.

'Especially for you,' he said good-humouredly and let us take them.

Thus, once more reunited with our faithful steeds, we were ready at last to go to Spain.

Or were we?

'There are no youth hostels in Spain,' Agnes, our camping guru, reminded us. 'And camping is extremely difficult.'

'In fact, if the Spanish police see a tent in a field, they think it's the beginning of an invasion, or maybe a revolution,' she added. People known to her family had been awakened while camping in Spain by police pointing pistols at them through the tent doorway.

'The Spanish roads are very rough,' she continued, no doubt thinking of all the punctures she would probably have to try and mend.

'We only need to go to Barcelona,' I suggested. Barcelona would be enough of Spain to allow us to include that country in our Grand European Tour. If we went by train and stayed at a cheap hotel there, we wouldn't need our bikes, I continued.

'Perhaps we could send them on ahead of us to a town on our route through France,' Esme put in, contributing the best idea of all.

And so this is what we did, although it was rather hard to be parted from our machines so soon after having waited for them for so long. We consulted the station indicator and a map of France. Eventually, we chose the town of Poitiers.

But to send our bikes ahead of us to Poitiers from Marseilles turned out to be a mammoth task. Forms had to be filled in, tickets bought, insurance paid. At ten minutes to twelve, we were still re-labelling our cycles.

Finally, as the clock struck midnight, we staggered – four Cinderellas, our arms filled with baggage, including tent – into the crowded train.

34

BARCELONA

We tried to doze beside our piled-up luggage on the train's corridor floor. From here we watched the sun rise above the Mediterranean sea – a rosy haze slowly extending its flush behind the clouds until daylight broke through, painting them a pinkish-yellow.

Eventually, a French girl offered me her seat while she went to the dining car. Then her friend offered Barbara hers. Later, a Frenchman, also going to eat, offered Agnes his, and a Spaniard offered his to Esme. But instead of trying to sleep, we began to talk.

'I wonder if we'll see Pete and John in Spain,' Barbara said about the two men we last saw in Luxembourg. 'You remember what that gypsy prophesied.'

'Not that I believed her, of course,' she added, trying to sound sceptical.

Suddenly, I saw it all. The penny dropped. What an old sly boots Barbara was. No wonder she'd been so insistent we go to Spain – but making out all the time that it was part of the general plan, which we were committed to accomplish. It was really because she had her eye on John and wanted to meet him again.

'You'll need a bit of luck,' I said, smiling to myself. 'I should think it would be like finding two needles in a haystack. For them to be there at exactly the same time and in the same place is most unlikely. If you really wanted to see them again, why didn't you arrange a proper meeting place and time?'

'Because we'd have been bound to miss them if we had,' Agnes put in wisely. 'Something would have gone wrong. It was better to leave it to chance. After all, we've been fairly lucky up to now.'

'Port Bou at the frontier is a sort of bottleneck,' Esme remarked reflectively. 'They're most likely to enter or leave Spain that way. The big question is – when?'

'I still think the chance of meeting them in Spain is very slight,' I commented, adding: 'We'll need too much luck – to be Fortune's favourites, in fact.' Meeting them again in Luxembourg had been a coincidence. To meet them in Spain would be a miracle.

However, fortune did favour us a bit at the frontier when a paternal porter in a long blue smock and black cap took us under his kindly wing.

It was still fairly early in the morning when I changed some money and we filled in more forms. The frontier officials only glanced cursorily at our passports. As at some of the other frontiers, they did not seem to notice Esme's damaged one. Our shabby baggage under the protective care of the elderly porter merely received a few scornful glances although many of the expensive-looking cases round us were opened and searched.

The next train we caught, which was to take us to Barcelona, was like the inside of a bus. Wooden seats, each holding three people, faced each other down the carriage. As on some Austrian trains, there was an outside platform where people could sit and watch the passing scenery.

The early morning mist had lifted now and it was bright enough to see how the countryside had changed. The lofty mountains seemed more rugged, wilder, with fewer cultivated plots than those of Italy and France. Fields of sunflowers flashed by, then tobacco and maize. We occasionally passed tiny impoverished villages, composed of groups of dusty, dilapidated houses, a church, a line of cypresses, and straggling olive trees.

Our train was a slow one, halting at every station. Or perhaps they should be called 'stopping-places', rather than stations, for there were no platforms. At one, a crowd of women sat on the ground, awaiting their train's arrival. Then these plump, chattering bodies, many carrying crates of chickens, or large shopping baskets, clambered aboard. They were followed by a few Civic Guards, quite smart in their grey-green uniforms and flat black hats, in sharp contrast to the groups of soldiers in dirty khaki, dusty boots and red-tasselled caps who clambered on after them.

At another station, a bearded beggar boarded the train and sang a wild and haunting song to the delight of the other passengers. They clapped and dropped coins into his grimy hat. He bowed, grinning, and sang again. But this time not so well, so there was no applause and no money. He shrugged his broad shoulders philosophically and climbed out at the next stop.

It was past two when our train finally drew into the dusty grey city of Barcelona.

And, as usual, there was the old problem of finding somewhere to stay. Our good friend Guilio, who'd been to Barcelona on business, had recommended a cheap hotel he'd used himself.

But unfortunately, according to the station map, its street was some distance from the station. As we had no bikes with us, it meant loading our baggage into one of the shabby yellow cabs that crawled around the entrance. Even more unfortunately, after it had rattled through the hot streets, we found that Guilio's recommended hotel was full up.

Still, we did have another string to our bow. A member of Agnes's Federal Union lived in Barcelona. She had been planning to contact him as soon as we'd settled ourselves into a hotel there.

But before she had a chance to find his address in her book, a slight, rat-faced man, who'd been watching our arrival – and disappointment – stepped out from a nearby alleyway.

'I take you to a good place,' he offered.

We turned to him uncertainly. We were very tired.

'He OK,' shouted our taxi driver, who had been waiting to see what we would do before he sped off.

'Perhaps he is.' But there was not much conviction in Agnes's voice.

The man raised a bony hand and beckoned us to follow him down a side-turning.

He led us through squalid streets, crowded with men. Some were sightless or one-legged; many sold watches, postcards or lottery tickets; others, swarthy and sinister, called out to us mockingly from house doorways as we passed by.

The *pension* was situated in a tall stone building above a rough café. We had to climb a dimly lit, paint-peeling staircase, past a barber's shop, to the floor above.

A small man, whose facial features made him look more Japanese than Spanish, surreptitiously opened the greasy door when we knocked.

'Room for four nice English ladies?' our self-appointed guide asked silkily, his tongue lingering on the word 'nice'.

The proprietor smiled widely, bowing very low in mock courtesy.

The room that he showed us was unsurprisingly dingy, furnished with four beds, covered with stained pink quilts, rickety chairs and a cracked wash-basin. However, its ornate ceiling bore witness to a grander past. Unfortunately, the fat cherubs playing amid roses decorating it were cut short by the tall walls.

Agnes sniffed. There was a strong smell of disinfectant.

'It's very clean,' our guide assured us, then added: 'You can wash.' He turned the rusty tap so that water dropped slowly into the discoloured basin.

'And don't we need to.' Barbara suddenly glimpsed herself in the mirror above the basin. We were filthy and dishevelled, looking like four bedraggled tramps.

But we were too tired to do anything about it just then. Without bothering to say any more, Agnes, Barbara and Esme collapsed onto three of the four beds.

It was left to me, the treasurer, to hand over ten pesetas out of the secret purse to our guide, hoping that it would be enough. After paying him ten pesetas and the driver thirty, it looked as if our stay in Barcelona would have to be a very short one.

Evidently he was satisfied for his thanks were profuse and he bowed himself out of the room, still smiling silkily.

Our hotel was situated in a creepy but fascinating part of Barcelona. After we'd woken up, got up and strolled into a nearby café, we felt quite scared. As in Marseilles, our table was surrounded but this time more gradually and furtively.

First came the beggars, then a one-eyed man turning the handle of a hurdy-gurdy, next a blind man, hawking candles, and lastly, two shaven-headed, barefoot boys. The shuffling and rather disreputable-looking waiter seemed unwilling to serve us and kept glancing uneasily over one shoulder.

'Let's move on,' Barbara suggested nervously as one grinning beggar held out two callused hands towards her.

So we quickly downed the sticky mixture dubiously called coffee, which the waiter had eventually brought us, and which I suspected might be doped, and wandered off down the narrow alleys which spread weblike through the mysterious, labyrinthine old city.

It was now dusk. Flickering gas jets on wall brackets cast shadows around us.

The shops, which had been closed when we arrived in Barcelona because it was afternoon, now had their blinds drawn and shutters open. I noticed a wet and smelly fish shop, a carpenter's, a shop selling charcoal in a gloomy basement, and a wine shop, whose dark, cavelike interior was stacked high with barrels.

The noise was terrific. Streets which had earlier held only a few people were now busy and crowded. This grew worse when we strolled out into the wider boulevards. There seemed to be people everywhere, even above us, looking down from the balconies of the tall houses, some of which were six storeys high.

There was an atmosphere of excited anticipation. Groups of young men in smart linen suits, gathered chiefly to watch the dark-eyed beauties swing past in their flowered dresses, were waiting expectantly. So now were the hawkers, the white uniformed sailors, the priests in their long black robes and soldiers in baggy khaki. Only the grey-uniformed Civic Guards stood diffidently aloof.

'An execution perhaps,' I suggested, sensing a drama.

'Nonsense!' a very hot Agnes snapped at me. 'More likely a fiesta.'

She was right, in a way. It was a rehearsal for a church festival which also served as an excuse for a celebration. Suddenly the murmurings of the crowd turned to cheers as the figures of a king and queen, the symbols of Barcelona, walked by on stilts, accompanied by two dwarves with enormous painted cardboard heads. This strange procession made its carnival way slowly down the street before stopping in front of a shop near the cathedral. The high wooden door swung open and they disappeared mysteriously inside.

However, this was not the end, only the beginning of the festivities. Life starts late in Barcelona where most people siesta during the hot afternoon. A small stage was set up nearby for a puppet show. Hawkers sold flags, windmills and sweets to the scrambling children. At every street corner there seemed to be a barrel organ playing and girls dancing. On all sides was noise – shouting, talking, singing and laughing.

This uproar seemed to go on right through the night. After we had strolled around, scrutinising faces – still hoping vaguely, but not really expecting, that we might come across Pete and John in the crowd – we returned to our shabby *pension*. Here we ate an enormous meal – it is customary to dine around nine in Barcelona – then retired to bed, but could not sleep because of the noise outside. The café below was particularly noisy. Doors slammed and men shouted, it seemed threateningly. Above the din we could hear the shrill hysterical voices of excited women.

35

PICNIC IN THE MOUNTAINS

'Today, we must try and find my contact in Barcelona,' Agnes said at breakfast, getting out her address book again. It was really an imperative, a necessity. None of us relished the thought of spending another night in this *pension*. It was too noisy, uncomfortable and dirty. We had all discovered red lumps on our bodies when washing in the cracked basin.

There was also the problem of the proprietor. Agnes, usually so benevolent and philanthropic towards her fellow humans, had taken an unexpected aversion to him. To make things really difficult for her, she seemed to fascinate him, so it was hard for her to ignore him. Perhaps for him it was the attraction of opposites, due to their different heights – he barely came past her waist; and their colourings – he so dark and she so fair.

At dinner the previous evening, he had come over to our table and tried to persuade her to accompany him to a bullfight, boasting that Barcelona had the best bullfights in Spain. To the great and very badly concealed amusement of us other three, he even tried to tempt her by acting out its drama.

First, he rushed round the room pretending that he was the bull; then he took the role of the matador, valiantly wielding his sword; next he became the bull again as it received the matador's final thrust, expiring on the floor. Agnes, who couldn't even bear insects being killed, sat stony-faced throughout this impressive demonstration.

So it was not long after breakfast that we were walking through the Plaza de Cataluña, Barcelona's vast square, and the junction of the old and new cities. Agnes confessed to us that she felt apprehensive about meeting this Spaniard who she'd only met twice before.

'He did say casually, "Do call in if you're ever in Barcelona," but I don't know what he'll say when he sees you three as well,' she added.

As we emerged into the Ramblas, Barcelona's most famous walk, a wide boulevard lined with arching plane trees, we were still looking around, vaguely expecting to see Pete and John. We also allowed ourselves, if very briefly, to examine some newspapers on one of the kiosks. For all we knew England might have been swallowed up by an earthquake. Then we visited the Rambla de los Estudios, the singing-bird market and the Rambla de las Flores, whose flower stalls brimmed with bunches of brightly coloured blooms.

Señor S – we all called him that because we couldn't pronounce his real name – worked in the administrative department of a large textile firm. His office was in a very tall building, almost a skyscraper, with high glass windows and doors.

Agnes need not have worried about our reception.

When he emerged into the large, quite luxuriously furnished waiting room, his rather heavy and solemn face relaxed into a warm smile.

'Agnes, what a nice surprise to see you.' He grasped her hand as if he'd known her all his life, then added, 'And your friends, too, of course.'

He was a big man, middle-aged, olive-skinned, and with an efficient, bustling manner. After Agnes had introduced him to Barbara, Esme and myself, it wasn't long before he asked her where we were staying. His large, luminous eyes rounded in horror when she told him. 'Oh, no! That part of the city is most unsuitable for respectable young women. Wait... I will take you somewhere better.'

Within minutes, we found ourselves hustled outside the tall glass doors and once more in a yellow cab. As a result of this journey, I learned the true cost of a taxi ride in Barcelona at that time. It was ten pesetas, as opposed to yesterday's thirty.

'But for a Spaniard it would not be so much,' Señor S told me sharply. 'Our drivers must be allowed to make a little profit on visitors.'

When we arrived back at the seedy *pension* above the café, the proprietor accepted our departure stoically, bowing obsequiously after I paid him. Señor S watched as I counted out the coins.

Our next hotel – small, clean and rather plain – was situated in a less crowded, insalubrious or exciting part of the city. Our cool all-white room had four iron-railed hospital-type beds and an old-fashioned telephone. Beyond the tall shuttered windows and down in the street below a hurdy-gurdy played incessantly, a constant reminder that we were still in Barcelona.

To our surprise – and delight – after we'd unpacked again and descended the narrow staircase to the hall, Señor S told us that he had just hired another taxi, and was going to show us Barcelona.

It was to the cathedral, night-black inside, that he took us first. Through the gloom Señor S pointed out the famous crucifix, fashioned, according to legend, from the mast of a Spanish galleon, which had played a glorious part in the battle of Lepanto. (This battle took place in the Gulf of Corinth off Greece in 1571.) Apparently, the tall pole had miraculously bent itself in order to avoid being hit by Turkish cannonballs, which had dropped uselessly into the sea. He also showed us the carved Moor's head, whose mouth was connected to an organ pipe, causing it to groan when played.

'Although Spain was occupied by the Moors for hundreds of years, Catalonia, of which Barcelona is the capital, was only occupied for one hundred years,' he told us proudly.

We passed but did not go into Gaudí's strange-looking and still unfinished church, whose ventilated spires, rising high above the city, resembled filigree or delicate lace tubes, tipped with stars.

'It was the work of a madman.' Although Señor S shook his head, he spoke with affectionate pride, adding: 'It was intended to be a cathedral for the poor, but as it was built by public subscription rather than official church funds, the money soon ran out.'

Although Barcelona was not typically Spanish, having once been the capital of a powerful and independent Catalonia, it nevertheless possessed the Pueblo Español, a village which was supposed to be the microcosm of everything Spanish, situated in the park. After a brief visit there, you could claim that you'd really seen Spain. The houses, streets and tiny squares represented the architectural styles to be found in the provinces and regions of Galicia, Seville, Andalucia, Aragon and any other part of the country you could think of.

We found it fascinating and spent so long there that it was evening when we finally drove to Tibidabo, the highest of the hills behind Barcelona.

Below and all around us was spread the city: the old, a maze of narrow streets, running higgledy-piggledy together; the new, blocks of high buildings and wide boulevards set out in neat squares. Beyond lay the old harbour, also merging old with new as tall masts mingled with funnels. Above them towered Christopher Columbus (1451–1506) on his pillar, gazing in the direction of his native Italy.

Señor S later took us back to his flat where we met his English wife, which explained how he spoke English so well. Although he continually told us how shocked he was by our 'long holiday', he informed us that he intended to take us to see Montserrat, outside Barcelona, the following day.

'But you will have to rise very early,' he warned. Then, briskly: 'I will call for you at your hotel about seven so that we can catch the bus.'

The phone between Agnes's and Esme's bed rang punctually at 6 a.m.

When the four of us trooped downstairs, we found Señor S waiting below in a very happy mood, wearing holiday-type clothes, including plimsoles and a cloth hat.

'No time for breakfast,' he told us. 'We have to catch the first bus.'

So we had to make do at a stall near the bus stop, where we bought buns and coffee.

The journey, which took perhaps two hours, was not very comfortable. We seemed to travel for miles along a bumpy, dusty road before the reddish-brown and grey pyramids, cones and ninepins – the fantastic outline of Montserrat, a mountain created 2,000 years ago by a volcanic eruption – came into view.

Señor S took us first to the monastery and village, which lay in a defile below, and then to the church. Here candles flickered above an ornate altar. The air reeked with incense. Brown-cowled monks chanted in the background as a priest bobbed up and down before the congregation, composed chiefly of black-veiled women.

'Play-acting!' Señor S snorted and shook his head, but more in sorrow than in anger.

As in Italy, it did not seem to matter if people walked around during the service, provided they made no noise. Señor S showed us the Black Virgin, which according to legend had been fashioned by St Luke and carried to Spain by St Peter. She was hidden in caves when the Moors attacked the country and was not taken out until it was safe for her to be shown again. The Benedictines had intended carrying her to Manresa, but when she was taken past the site of the old church, she became too heavy to move. This was taken as a signal that she wanted to remain in her old home, so the monks built a new church there.

'Most likely they were too tired to walk any further,' Señor S commented dryly.

The superstitious people, although very poor, had given her some of their most valuable possessions. This curious figure on the pedestal behind the altar was bedecked in costly vestments. She also had a wardrobe which contained many dresses and reels of material. Her wristwatches, brooches and bracelets were stored in the sacristy nearby.

By the time we left the church, it was midday again. Señor S decided we should buy food for our picnic. He seemed to have a mighty appetite. He made me buy quantities of cold meat, fish, bread, butter and fruit at a shop in the village, also two bottles of wine, some of which he insisted we drank before climbing on the funicular.

The effect of the wine and the swinging funicular made us four feel dizzy, especially as Señor S urged us to examine the rocks as we swung close to the cliffs. I had a blurred impression of little stones stuck together, but it apparently held a variety of fossilised remains, such as leaves and shells.

We all felt relieved when finally we reached the station at the top, then tramped down a path to a cool place under the trees.

We soon realised that although the hardworking Señor S repeatedly told us how shocked he was by our 'long holiday', he was also very envious, for he loved picnicking.

'For happiness, only three things are required – freedom, the open air and art,' he told us solemnly before stretching himself out on the ground.

We could not help wondering about freedom in Spain, which was then so obviously a dictator-run country. We would have been blind not to have noticed the pictures and posters about General Franco in Barcelona, or not to have been aware of all the uniformed police and armed soldiers, so continually on watch in the streets. We had not liked to question him about this in case we were overheard and got him into trouble.

'Barcelona has always been the home of revolution.' Señor S continued his homily from his prone position, his voice tinged with pride. It was probably safe for him to air his opinions there – so high up, hidden behind trees and away from the crowds. 'It is Spain's most enlightened city: the country's only hope. Franco doesn't dare visit us here. He knows only too well that a muzzled dog can still growl.'

After this outburst Señor S fell asleep. He was a big man and his breathing heavy. His stomach, resembling a mountain halfway down his body, rose and fell like the swell of the sea. His sombre features looked dignified, almost regal, as he slept.

Later, when it was cooler again and we felt less exhausted, Señor S led us higher along a rough road and up steps to a lookout place. From here was a magnificent view of the extraordinary and grotesque shaped peaks.

When we finally arrived back at Barcelona that evening, it seemed as if all the young people had taken to the streets, ignoring the traffic and the crowds. But it was not a revolution. They had placed themselves in rings and were clapping their hands and stamping their feet to the rhythm of flutes and drums.

'They are doing the sardana, a Catalan dance,' Señor S told us as we stopped to watch. 'You can try if you like. Anyone can join in.'

So we did, but not very successfully. The steps were more intricate than they looked and very difficult to follow.

'It is not a dance learned easily by foreigners,' Señor S told us comfortingly when we eventually, breathlessly, rejoined him.

He took us back to our hotel, whisking us past an altar, where priests were selling candles and packets of sweets, near the cathedral.

'I am travelling south for my firm tomorrow, so I won't be able to see you again,' he told us outside the hotel, adding that

that he hoped we had enjoyed our short visit to Spain and would successfully complete the rest of our tour.

We were sorry that this would be the last time we would see this big, friendly, good-natured Spaniard. We could not help wondering how long it would be before he went on another such glorious picnic.

36

TOWARDS POITIERS

This was our last day in Barcelona and in Spain, too: the day that we were to catch the train to France and start on the last leg of our tour. We had done well. We had almost accomplished our mission, and would finally finish it after we'd retrieved our bikes at Poitiers.

Our phone was rung by reception even earlier than it had been the previous morning. Even so, and in spite of the fact that we got to the station as soon as it was humanly possible, our platform was already crowded with people. We had to fight our way past baskets, boxes and crates towards the carriages.

Esme and I were the first to clamber aboard. It wasn't so much a question of finding a seat as a space that would hold four standing bodies and their baggage. We still felt sleepy and tired out from yesterday's excursion, as well as our other early risings.

'It's goodbye to Spain,' I yawned. 'And goodbye to finding Pete and John. So much for the gypsy's prophecy.'

'Hey!' Esme grabbed my arm. 'Look...' she said excitedly.

We were surrounded by Spaniards, mostly peasants, noisy, perspiring and poor, and a few soldiers. Through the mass of people, I glimpsed two others who might be tourists like ourselves. But they were facing away from us, looking in another direction.

'It's their backs, I'm sure!' Esme exclaimed. 'Those khaki shirts, that red handkerchief...'

Yes, I decided, they certainly were familiar.

Suddenly they turned so that we could see their faces. One was dark, bearded; the other red-skinned, pale-haired. Both looked doleful.

It couldn't be. And yet, amazingly, it was Pete and John!

Oh, blessed gypsy! We were Fortune's favourites, after all.

The other two saw them. Agnes, when she straightened up from stooping over our black basket and Barbara, turning with her arms filled with luggage.

But as the four of us stared, scrutinising them more carefully, we saw that there was something unusual about their appearance.

The two men were standing on the platform in their bare feet.

'Hello there!' Pete's face, suddenly scrubbed clean of its sombre expression, lit up with pleased surprise, as did John's.

'What's happened to your sandals?' an amazed, nay, delighted Barbara, asked.

'Oh, those!' Pete, glancing down at his bare, dirty feet tried to sound casual. 'We slept rough near here last night. Although we put our sandals between us and the rucksacks for safety, some light-fingered character must have crept up and nabbed them. They'd gone when we woke up.'

It was mean of us, of course, but we four couldn't help laughing at their awful predicament. They'd been so scornful, so mocking about our cycling and camping round Europe. Our tour to them had been one great joke. And yet, fingers crossed (we still had a bit further to go) nothing of ours had been stolen.

'Proper pilgrims, aren't you?' I couldn't help shouting at them through the carriage window.

'But you can't walk barefoot. Spanish roads are terrible,' Barbara exclaimed, horrified, remembering yesterday's bus journey.

It was Agnes, our ever resourceful leader, who came to their aid in the end. She suddenly remembered a pair of sandals she'd worn out and which she'd eventually had to tie on to her feet with some red tape she'd found when 'scanning' the ground. These had attracted so much unwelcome attention that we other three had first begged then ordered her to throw them away.

Luckily for everyone, she had frugally kept them, just in case. She was able to dig down into her panniers, then wave them triumphantly aloft.

'They might just fit you,' she said hopefully.

Pete gratefully fixed them under his dusty feet. They fitted. Just. Agnes, being so tall, had large feet for a girl. Surprisingly the lurid tapes blended with his kerchief. They might have been made for each other. Anyway, he was too relieved to have something to put under his feet to bother about appearances.

Then Barbara brought out a pair of thick socks for John. They were men's socks, which she'd borrowed from our brother. These plus some spare soles we still had, fixed on with laces from Barbara's heavy walking shoes, enabled him also to be shod.

'Where are you off to now?' I heard my sister ask John quickly. Our train was almost ready to start. While she and Agnes had been seeing to their feet, Esme and I, with the help of a nearby Spaniard, had managed to pile all our luggage inside the train.

'Madrid. I want to visit the Prada. I've an uncle who lives there who'll lend me some money,' we heard John shout back at her.

Our train was beginning to move very slowly and Esme and I were urging the other two to climb aboard. There was a terrible crush of people. We were having great difficulty in keeping any sort of space free for them to stand in.

'Do you want your sandals back?' Pete was now running alongside the train.

'No, I was going to throw them away...' Agnes was shouting generously, still half in and half out of the train, when I gave her a sharp dig.

'For goodness sake, say you want them back. Give him your address.'

So she wrote it down swiftly on the back of an old hotel bill, balancing it on the carriage window. Alas, she was too late. Before she'd finished the train had gathered speed, leaving Pete and John far away from us, down the platform.

'I take it, Miss,' a dark hand emerged from the forest of hands waving round us and Agnes thrust it swiftly forward. The paper fluttered away out of sight.

Did he receive it? In the distance, I thought I perceived one hairy arm, a luxuriant tree among lesser, shorter plants, waving frantically. Was that scrap of white paper our hotel bill wavering above them? It was difficult to be sure.

Our journey, so cramped and uncomfortable, was made slightly more bearable by talking to a Spaniard who spoke a little English and had helped Esme and me with the luggage.

He was a small man, dark and sad-eyed as if he had suffered. I noticed that he was wearing a tiny cross on the lapel of his brown suit. As he had helped us and seemed to be dropping with fatigue, we made room for him on our panniers, even taking it in turn to stand, so that he would have more space to sit and rest.

We discovered that his weariness was chiefly due to a pilgrimage that he'd made to Montserrat. He told us that he'd been captured during the Civil War by the 'Reds' and that when he knew he was to be shot, he vowed that should his life be spared, he would make a pilgrimage through Spain on foot to the Black Virgin. He *was* spared, 'most miraculously', he said. This had been the first chance in a difficult life to carry out his pledge.

We left him at Toulouse, where we had to change trains. And what a relief it was to escape from that crowded carriage.

234

Toulouse did not make much of an impression on us except that it seemed to be built out of a reddish-brown brick, and that, according to our Spanish friend, it was known as the 'Red City' and was notorious for its revolutionary fervour.

Spain now lay behind us. We were in France. Dear old France! Although it was still very hot, the heat seemed less violently oppressive than it had been in Spain. I changed some money at the bank; pesetas into francs. How tired I was of all these different currencies. Also, by now, we didn't have much money left.

'From now on it's camping again. No more hotels for us,' I told the other three firmly.

The next train we caught took us to Bordeaux, a slow, tedious journey, so that we did not arrive there until about ten o'clock at night. So much for camping again! Although we had our tent with us, it was too late, dark and difficult to start looking for a site.

'There are trains leaving Bordeaux all through the night,' I told them, scanning the destination board. 'Suppose we just go on to Poitiers where we sent the bikes?'

Agnes, Barbara and Esme agreed.

'A carriage seat will probably be just as comfortable as sleeping on the ground,' Esme remarked. 'Then we can start our cycling again.'

'That's if our bikes have arrived,' Barbara put in speculatively.

This was something we had yet to find out.

When we arrived at Poitiers, the official on duty there was quite indignant after Agnes enquired uncertainly about them. It seemed that she had challenged the good name of French Railways by supposing that they might not have reached the station. He led us stiffly up the platform into a yard smelling of fish and littered with parcels.

'*Voilà!*' He made an abrupt gesture.

And there, spotted with sawdust, staid and angular (even Esme's) amongst others of newer and gayer design, stood our four faithful companions of some 3,000 miles of travelling. Oh, joy! We almost hugged their dear handlebars.

It was very early in the morning and we felt quite cold. This was not only because of the hour but also because we had come so much further north. Later, when in the waiting room where we changed into the warmer clothes we'd worn in Belgium and the first part of Germany, we were dismayed to find that they were now too big for us. We seemed to have shrunk.

'I must have lost pounds,' Esme wailed. The poor girl could hardly keep her skirt up.

Nevertheless, revived by black coffee and some buns, we set off quite cheerfully on our bikes again, through Poitiers and out into the French countryside, now on the very last stage of our long journey.

The air felt gloriously fresh. Rays from the morning sun danced lightly over the grey roof tiles of the houses. The countryside seemed beautiful. It was so serene and peaceful. The bushes, trees and grass were bright green after the arid dryness of Spain.

'Just like England,' I said.

To begin with, we four seemed to take on new wings. But this didn't last. As we had been travelling one long day and night, natural tiredness had to have its way. Eventually we began to flag.

Even so, we managed to ride about fifteen miles before we stopped and then it was chiefly to buy some food at a little village shop. After this halt, we rode on awhile until we came to a field, which looked as if it might be a suitable resting place, about halfway up a leafy lane.

Here a yawning Agnes and Barbara spread out our groundsheet over the spiky grass. We ate slowly, then gradually collapsed beneath a warmer ten o'clock sun. And nothing, not even an earthquake, would have awakened us.

Yet we could not camp in this pleasant field. Although great freedom is allowed to campers in France – a tent could be erected almost anywhere – Agnes had been too well trained by her father to break Camping Club rules. There was no house nearby at which we could ask permission. Nor, when we continued our journey, was there any place we could obtain drinking-water.

However, drinking-water, as such, we were soon to discover did not seem to exist in this fair, green land.

Later that evening, when we drew up at a farmhouse near Châtellerault, the farmer, when asked for drinking-water, took us to a pool.

'*L'eau potable*?' Agnes asked unbelievingly, for the water lay very still and an empty bottle was floating on its surface. When Barbara and I looked closer, we could see that the bottom was swarming with crawling insects.

'*Potable*,' the farmer assured us emphatically. And to prove that it was really all right, he scooped some up in his hands and drank noisily.

We weren't convinced.

'He must be immune to the effects of drinking bad water,' Barbara declared. She carefully boiled all that she took from the pool. We did not want to become ill on this the very last stage of our tour.

37

THE LOIRE VALLEY AND HOME

We were now very close to the famous French Châteaux Country, in whose green hills and valleys the kings and nobles of France had once built their castles and palaces.

Tours is an agricultural and industrial centre named after its abundance of towers. Even then, not so very long after the war, it seemed a very busy city. When we arrived there the following day, we found we had a job to weave our way through its traffic to the countryside. Once there, we couldn't find a suitable site: most of the land seemed to be laid out in neat vegetable gardens, vineyards or orchards, or was too sloping to pitch a tent.

Eventually, we decided we'd do what a French friend had advised us to do when in difficulty in France: ask the mayor! Here the mayor of a place is an important personage, who can accomplish all sorts of unexpected things. All that we wanted on this particular occasion was for him to tell us where we could pitch our tent.

A policeman guided us to the local mayor's house, where we interrupted him at his evening meal. Even so, he was not at all put out by our request and politely escorted us to a playing field.

At first, we thought this was where he intended us to camp, amongst the goalposts and jumping stands. But no, not at all. Instead, he led us to the sports pavilion and unfastened the door.

'*Voilà!*' he gestured dramatically. Inside was to be our dormitory for the night.

'It's not such a bad place, really,' Esme remarked later.

'We've slept in plenty worse,' I put in.

'At least there's electric light – and chairs and benches to sit on,' Agnes commented.

'And I can cook our evening meal on a proper table with room to spare.' Barbara looked pleased. At least she wouldn't have to stoop like she did in the tent.

We built ourselves beds out of the chairs, which we placed in two lines, facing each other – although we would probably have done better if we'd used the floor. We had to lie very still. Each time one of us moved the chairs slid apart, leaving head and feet precariously balanced.

This sports pavilion, which was also used as a village hall, had posters and advertisements stuck around the walls. For our greater safety, and so that we shouldn't be disturbed, Agnes locked the door with the mayor's key. Barbara, in particular, was rather on edge. Once in the night, she sat up so suddenly that her chairs shot apart, almost landing her on the floor.

'There's a face at the window,' she screamed hysterically.

Agnes, with me close behind clutching our knife, unlocked and swung open the door, to find – nobody! The face at the window was truly villainous, but only the reflection of a horror movie poster in the glass.

The last stage of our journey through the garden of France – cycling alongside the broad, flat Loire, shadowed dreamily by trees – was perhaps the most peaceful part of the whole tour. The luminous Loire, so shining and unpredictable, is the longest river in France at about 634 miles. It is a fickle river, sometimes angry, sometimes lazy. In autumn and in winter it can flood.

The area known as the Loire Valley and the Châteaux Country, though, lies only between Angers and Gien. Our favourite château was the one at Chenonceaux, a long pale residence at the end of an avenue of trees. Below its arches flowed the river Cher like a natural moat. In olden times, courtiers would fish from the tall windows above.

We also visited the massive fortress at Amboise, whose history is grisly, and the château at Blois, once the home of the French court and perhaps the best known of all in the Loire Valley. Our tour ended in its great pillared Salle de Généraux, where the French Assembly had met, prior to the revolution.

Our Grand Tour, too, was almost complete. Not only were we coming to the end of our money, but it was likely we would only be able to spend one more night in our lopsided tent.

That evening we drew up on our cycles at a farm outside a village. When Agnes asked the white-whiskered, red-faced owner if we could camp on his land, he instructed his small grandson to take us to a field, which lay alongside the railway line.

'Why can't we put our tent where we like? Everyone else does,' I grumbled.

'Mustn't break Camping Club rules,' Esme replied mockingly.

This particular place was most unsuitable. It was dirty and noisy. Especially noisy. The vibration caused by the trains rattling past shook our tent so badly that the mended pole eventually gave way and collapsed in the night.

Barbara, Esme and I, worn out from that day's cycling and sightseeing, barely stirred in our sleeping bags. We blamed Agnes and her ridiculous rules for our being there at all. So we let her get on with it. She was nearest the pole and had a hard struggle to prevent the tent caving in on us.

'And still those trains keep coming by,' we heard her wail indignantly. It was as if she expected the driver, seeing our predicament in the swaying tent, to stop his train, and maybe come to our rescue.

'It's the last time we'll be able to use this tent,' she prophesied as she carefully rewound the string about the cracked pole.

The old cathedral town of Chartres was our final destination before catching a train first to Paris, then Calais, our port of departure. We had planned the last part of the tour some time ago. I had carefully laid aside some traveller's cheques to cover the cost of our train fare as well as enough money for our boat tickets home.

As usual, we arrived in the evening. The sun was setting. A silvery moon swung high in a rosy sky, illuminating the outline of the tall cathedral spires, which loomed above the red and grey rooftops.

It was beautiful enough to make us stop awhile on the old bridge we were crossing. Reeds sticking out of the flowing shallow water put me in mind of the porcupine quills represented in the royal crest of Louis XII at Blois. The old houses, their stone walls lapped by water, reminded us all of Venice.

Our broken tent pole forced us to stay the night at the youth hostel, a very dilapidated place, although to Barbara's delight, it did have quite a good kitchen.

As the next day was Sunday, we were awakened by the sound of cathedral bells tolling. While we knew we should catch the train to Paris as soon as possible, it would have been sacrilege to leave Chartres without visiting its famous cathedral.

We wandered inside, passing dim shapes sitting with bowed heads. As in Italy and Spain, no one seemed to object to our exploring its interior while a service was in progress. 'A fitting end to our tour,' I remarked to Esme. 'I suppose like pilgrims of long ago, we should deliver thanks for its safe completion.'

'There's still Paris, don't forget, and the crossing. Anything can happen to us,' Esme reminded me darkly.

The cathedral was a place of contrasts: sombre grey pillars and glittering candles; in one corner, a tourist crouching over his camera; in another, a black-veiled woman praying before a solitary candle. It was very dim inside. Then suddenly the overcast sky outside cleared, releasing the sun from the clouds to stream through the famous stained glass windows, flooding the interior with soft pink, mauve, green and blue dancing lights.

Chartres cathedral is truly a people's church. After it was burned down in the twelfth century, it was rebuilt over a period of 18 years; quite quick for those days. All sorts of people – princes, paupers, clergy, traders, artisans and peasants – gave money or labour to help in its reconstruction.

The pictures in the windows were of the thirteenth century. The figures of the prophets, apostles and martyrs occupied the highest positions and were to be gazed at from afar. Some windows glorified a particular trade, such as a furrier offering pieces of stuff to a rich client, or a water-carrier pouring green water into a blue vase. The secret of how the famous limpid *bleu de Chartres*, particularly beautiful at sunset, was made was lost for hundreds of years. Other windows told stories from the Bible and the lives of saints.

'*Our tour was rather like a story too, but one which we made up as we went along. We never knew what was going to happen to us next,*' I wrote in my diary.

Of Paris, however, we only saw a small corner and my impressions were sketchy. Our financial position only enabled us to stay there a very short time.

Barbara reminded me and the other two that we had to be home in time for our brother's wedding. We had collected a letter from the Poste Restante in Florence confirming that it was to take place on the twentieth of August.

'We've still got to get our bridesmaids' dresses fitted. We've both lost weight, so there'll have to be alterations. We must leave Calais by the fifteenth of August,' she told us firmly.

When we did finally arrive at Calais on that day, we all felt it hard to believe that our tour was really over. It was sad in a way. Our long journey had now passed into memory. On the other hand, it was a relief that we'd done it. It was finished. It was an achievement we had brought off. There was no prize, of course. But it was proof positive that girls could do things if they tried.

However, the big surprise was still to come.

As we struggled aboard the ferry with our equipment, I thought I saw a vision, a mirage perhaps. I was sure I glimpsed two tall, tanned, familiar figures standing near the gangway. But I knew it couldn't be. I glanced quickly at Agnes, Barbara and Esme, but their three heads were bowed as they heaved their baggage up the gangway. I rubbed my eyes and looked again. They'd disappeared. 'It's my imagination,' I thought. 'It does sometimes play tricks when I'm hot and tired.'

I said nothing about it to the other three. Then I forgot about it in the palaver of trying to get ourselves organised. About half an hour later, when the ferry was rolling around on the slight swell, the four of us made our way down to the café to buy some tea and biscuits. I was delighted to find that I had just enough French francs to do this.

This time all four of us saw them. It was no vision. It really was Pete and John. Only John was wearing a very old pair of shoes over the socks that Barbara had given him (we learned later that he'd found them in a dustbin!).

You can imagine our excitement.

'But how?' I especially was mystified. They were supposed to be in Madrid. 'It's too much of a coincidence. It must be witchcraft,' I said.

'Not really.' John was grinning as if it were a tremendous joke. 'Your sister told us that you had to be home in time for a wedding and that you'd probably be leaving Calais on the fifteenth. We worked out that you'd probably be on this boat.'

'Old smarty boots following us around with your notebook. You don't see and hear everything.' Barbara thumped me on the back. 'I told John our probable movements when you others were too busy to hear.'

'We've been following you through France,' John told us. 'When we got to Chartres, they told us you'd just left for Paris.'

'What about Madrid?' Agnes asked.

'We decided to give it a miss,' John answered.

'We figured a country with people in it mean enough to pinch your shoes while you were asleep wasn't worth seeing anyway,' Pete added.

So that was it; the end of the tour. It was also the end of my diary. The six of us returned to England together. Travelling in the way we did by cycling and camping had put us more in touch with the life of the countries through which we passed. It had forced us to try out and add to what little of the languages we knew. Admittedly our lack of money and method of travel had created difficulties, but help was usually readily given, sometimes amazingly so. We had learned that people, whatever their nationality – even ex-enemies – were good at heart. Perhaps the fact that Britain was on the winning side in the war, and assisted in the liberation of Europe, gave us a certain kudos.

We also learned to cooperate with each other and tolerate each other's foibles. Would we ever do the same thing again? Maybe. Eastern Europe would be difficult because of the Iron Curtain, then the separation of the democracies from the communist countries. But there was still Scandinavia in the northern reaches to visit...

EPILOGUE

The year is 2005 – over fifty years since our European expedition.

I am sitting in the same room of the same flat in which the four of us gave our farewell party to friends and relatives before setting off on our Grand Tour of Europe. I don't think our guests thought we would get very far. At the time everyone thought we were slightly mad, as I suppose we were. Nowadays it would be different. Young backpackers go off to the ends of the earth visiting the most dangerous, exciting and exotic places. I suppose you could say that we were ahead of our time. Maybe even pioneers.

Many things in the world have changed since 1951. And not, I think, for the better. Even so, the flat is considerably more comfortable than it was then. The occupants have changed, too. I now share the place with a niece, my sister's daughter; and a friend, a retired nurse.

There were no great repercussions as a result of our tour. Agnes found that she wasn't all that keen on Pete, who returned to Australia. As for John, things turned out differently there, too. Although we celebrated our reunion on board the boat, we went our separate ways at Dover. Barbara and I had to return home quickly to be in time for our brother's wedding. Agnes and Esme came too as they were to be guests. We were all in time – very brown and considerably thinner. Barbara and I had to have our bridesmaids' dresses speedily altered as we'd both lost so much weight.

Then, shortly after the wedding, Barbara was off on her course where she was to train to be a youth employment officer and where she met and fell in love with her husband-to-be,

John Ward. She never actually became a youth employment officer herself – her husband had the only such job going in the area in which they settled. Instead she had three children and now has five grandchildren. She took up painting later in life, distributing her works around her family – I have five. Unfortunately she had two strokes in her seventies and is now almost immobile but is looked after by her patient and devoted husband.

Agnes returned to Federal Union but left after she and I took a cycle-camping tour of Denmark, Sweden and Norway. She obtained a job in a building firm where she helped Barry Bucknell of fifties and sixties TV fame with his DIY programmes. She later worked at Harefield Hospital where she assisted on various health projects. She was never very career-orientated but loved to help people. She had many friends. Sadly, she died of lung cancer about twelve years ago.

Esme returned to secretarial work, but she had developed itchy feet. Although Gustavo, the austere Italian lawyer, did come to London to visit her, she had other ideas. She went to live and work in Canada for a few years. On her return, she worked for a while in the production department of a publishing firm and later set up a successful theatrical agency with an old school friend. She is now retired and lives in Somerset.

As for me, I typed out my diary and wrote and sold ten articles on our trip. I left teaching and in 1953 went on the afore-mentioned tour of Scandinavia with Agnes. After several jobs in the media, I became a travel writer, publishing six travel guides and innumerable articles. I am still working, and there is no doubt that our Grand European Tour laid the foundation of my travel writing career.

OTHER SUMMERSDALE TITLES

EDWARD ENFIELD
GREECE
ON MY WHEELS

summersdale *travel*

Greece On My Wheels

Edward Enfield

£7.99 Paperback

Two enchanting explorations of Greece by bicycle.

Mounted on his trusty steed, Edward explores the beauty and history of the Pelopponese in a travelogue that combines wit, charm and scholarship. Returning to Greece to follow in the footsteps of the Romantic poet Lord Byron, Edward's second trip sees him pedalling around the great historic sites of Epirus as he completes his own mini odyssey.

'displays genuine empathy with his surroundings, an infectious admiration for ancient Greek culture, and occasional flashes of wry wit, to provide a memorably satisfying read'

The Bookseller

'full of humour and wonderful depictions of the wild beauty and fascinating people of Greece – all seen from the saddle of his trusty steed, no mean feat for a man approaching 70!'

The Oldie

'Enfield not only impresses – he informs and delights'

Wanderlust Mag

'the most charming travelogue I've read this year. Mr Enfield (young Harry's father) takes the reader on a cycling tour, a history lesson and a literary safari that combines old world wit and charm with a sweeping breadth of knowledge. This volume should be on every creative writing course syllabus as an example of travel writing at its best'

Paul Blezard, Oneword Radio

THE SEA AHEAD

From Cape Wrath to the Riviera on foot

by the bestselling author of *The Sea on our Left*

SHALLY HUNT

The Sea Ahead

From Cape Wrath to the Riviera on foot

Shally Hunt

£7.99 Paperback

What would you do if you suddenly had all the time in the world?

For **Shally Hunt** and her husband Richard, one week at home was enough before they set off on a 2,300-mile walk from Scotland to Nice, carrying their simple needs on their backs. The couple camped wild in some of the loneliest places in Scotland, encountering searing heat in Lorraine and the Vosges and wild thunder storms in the High Alps. Along the way they met some fascinating characters, like the medium with a penchant for local liqueurs and the man who completed the Tour des Alpes Maritimes on one leg.

Shally and Richard reached Nice with their sense of humour and marriage still intact – a remarkable achievement, for their journey was no ordinary walk.

PETER KERR

Thistle Soup

summersdale *travel*

Thistle Soup

Peter Kerr

£7.99 Paperback

A brimming and lively broth of rural characters, drunken ghosts, bullocks in the bedrooms and country superstitions.

East Lothian is 'The Garden of Scotland' and the setting of this delightfully idiosyncratic story of country life. Often hilarious, always heartfelt and at times sad, here is unfolded the ups and downs of four generations of one farming family from the northerly Orkney Isles, who move to the little farm of Cuddy Neuk in the south of Scotland just before the outbreak of the Second World War. A young Peter, the peedie boy who sets his heart on filling his somewhat eccentric grandfather's straw-lined wellies, grows up to run the family farm and become a farmer father to his own sons, putting his ability to see the funny side of things to good use, as adversities crop up with an intriguing reality...

www.summersdale.com